The Goddess
Effect-Revealed

The Goddess Effect-Revealed

Goddess The Book

Lori Snyder

BALBOA.
PRESS
A DIVISION OF HAY HOUSE

Balboa Press books may be ordered through booksellers or by contacting:

Balboa Press
A Division of Hay House
1663 Liberty Drive
Bloomington, IN 47403
www.balboapress.com
1 (877) 407-4847

Printed in the United States of America.

ISBN: 978-1-4525-8433-1 (sc)
ISBN: 978-1-4525-8434-8 (e)

Library of Congress Control Number: 2013918453

Balboa Press rev. date: 4/3/2014

To my beloved Grandmother Lillian, who taught me through her amazing inner strength and love, how to be strong when life lessons hit.

And to my beautiful daughters Holli and Ashley, who have been such a joy and happiness in my life. Words cannot express. how proud I am, as I watch each of you grow into your unique selves, both with such wonderful values, and heart's full of goodness. I love you both tons, way beyond what could ever be expressed in words. My wish is that this book is one in which you can tap into, to gather whatever it is you wish, at different points in your lives. And of course, to my future grandchildren, and great grandchildren, I love you all a bunch already, and give you my gift of wisdom within these pages.

And to my Mother, who always made sure throughout our childhood that my sisters and I always had an abundance of love, care and happiness.

Contents

Chapter One: See-Believe-Become

Quotes to Ponder

Imagination is everything. It is the preview of life's coming attractions.

~ Albert Einstein

What power this is I cannot say. All that I know is that it exists.

~ Alexander Graham Bell

Whatever your mind can conceive and can believe, it can achieve.

~ Napoleon Hill

Main Scoop

Are you wishing for a richer more fulfilling life, filled with abundance? Even with life's up's and down's, if you are not satisfied with your current economic or life situation, the change you desire is possible!

Surely you've heard the axiom, *"If you keep doing what you've been doing, you'll keep getting what you've got."* In order for things to change, you need to do something differently.

Doing things differently starts with a change in your thoughts. When you change your thinking, you automatically change your actions to be in alignment with your new thoughts and attitudes.

But how do you think differently to attract what you desire? Do you just wish for it really hard and then assume that you'll do the right thing?

No! Not at all! In fact, wishing too hard can push it farther and farther away from you! I'll explain why in a moment.

On the contrary, there are tangible things you can *do* every day to change your thoughts and your life!

> **"Men do not attract that which they want,**
> **but that which they are."**
>
> **~ James Allen in "As A Man Thinketh"**

When you demonstrate the life you want, you'll attract it back toward you.

Granted, you can't just leap from your life into your *dream life* in a single step, but you can build the bridge that enables you to cross over in the shortest possible time.

Start out with some conscious actions and do them consistently every day. These actions become habits and help you ingrain new thoughts and attitudes into your subconscious.

These new thoughts and attitudes are the ones that will help you attract the life you desire. They make up the mindset that requires you to act in accordance with the life you want.

❖ Do you desire financial freedom?

❖ Could your relationships use some more passion? Or, are you hoping to be in a loving relationship?

❖ What about your physical self? Are you satisfied with your body, hair, and overall style?

❖ Do you feel joy and happiness in your life? Do you want more?

You can make all these things happen! All it takes is a commitment to bring this abundance into your life and the follow-up actions to make it a reality.

The following pages will guide you through specific action steps you can take to attract the life you desire. Engage in these actions every day, and soon you'll realize the life of joy and happiness you've always wanted.

> *"We are what we think...*
> *All that we are, arises with our thoughts.*
> *With our thoughts we make our world."*
>
> *~ **Buddha***

Your Perception is Your Reality

Is your glass half full or half empty?

How you perceive the events in your life both big and small, not only shows your underlying mindset about your life, but also plays the most important role in whether you ever reach your goals.

Let's use the glass to demonstrate this concept. Imagine the glass has tasty lemonade in it, and you really like lemonade. What are your thoughts when you see it?

If you're optimistic, of course you see it as half full. You may have thoughts like these:

- ❖ *"Oh, boy! I've got some delicious lemonade to quench my thirst!"*
- ❖ As you reach for the glass, you feel anticipation and gratitude for this good and tasty drink.
- ❖ Your thoughts are happily focused on what you *have* in this moment, not on what you *lack.*

The simple joy of some nice, cool lemonade and the good feelings that go along with it cause your brain to send out energy that vibrates in harmony with good things, and *attracts more good things back to you.*

Now look at what happens when you're a pessimist and see the glass as half empty. Your thoughts may be closer to these:

- ❖ *"Oh, great* (sarcastically). *I'm so thirsty and all I've got is half a glass of lemonade."*
- ❖ As you reach for the glass, you feel dissatisfaction. You wish you had more.
- ❖ Your thoughts are on what you lack.

Not only do you miss out on any enjoyment from the lemonade, but your mind sends out energy that vibrates in harmony with dissatisfaction and lack. What do you think you'll attract back to you? More things to be unhappy about and more lack!

This also explains why wishing for something too hard can push it away from you. *When you're wishing for something you don't have, you're focusing on your lack of it.* Focusing on your *lack* of it only attracts *more lack* of it back to you!

This simple glass of lemonade shows how your perception is your reality. *Two different people can have two totally different experiences from the same circumstance.* One person's experience adds to the happiness of a joyful life and the other's adds more problems to their unsatisfying existence.

It also explains why some people can make lemonade (and enjoy it) when life hands them lemons, while some just can't.

When you apply this lesson to your own life, what do you find? Are you attracting good things or more lack? Could you use some ways to change your mindset?

"Life is the movie you see through your own unique eyes.
It makes little difference what's happening out there.
It's how you take it that counts."

~ **Dr. Dennis Waitley** from *"The Winner's Edge"*

Live "In The Moment"

Dr. Joe Vitale, motivational speaker and author, has said many times, *"The fastest way to get where you want to be is to be happy with where you are."* This seems almost contradictory, but, in fact, it reveals a great truth.

The more *"good vibrations"* you send out, the more good things you attract back to you to be happy about. One of the best ways to be sending out good vibrations consistently, is to live in the moment.

What does this mean? It means that you remain in the now – not yesterday or tomorrow. You treat each moment as the precious thing that it is and *enjoy it to its fullest.* You immerse yourself fully in the moment.

Living in the moment can help you to:

❖ Reduce stress
❖ Relieve worry about the future
❖ Eliminate anguish about the past
❖ Enable you to brush away distractions and focus on your task at hand
❖ Bring more passion to your relationships
❖ Allow you to leap toward achieving your goals faster than you ever thought possible

❖ Let you enjoy the peace, happiness, and contentment of a fulfilling life

Here are some action steps you can take to help you live in the moment:

1. **Watch the movie "The Peaceful Warrior."** This movie will bring you a great understanding about living in the moment.

   It's based on events in the life of champion gymnast Dan Millman. After a tragic accident paralyzes him, his doctors say he'll never walk again. With the help of his mentor who teaches him to live in the moment, Dan not only walks, but competes as a world champion gymnast once again!

   It's a true story and reveals exceptionally well how living in the moment can truly change your life for the better. As his mentor teaches him the philosophy and techniques, so, too, will you learn.

2. **Take time to stop and smell the roses.** This applies not only to enjoying the simple, good things in life, but it also applies to *literally* taking the time to notice what's around you so you can take pleasure from what your senses bring you.

   ❖ Notice the physical world around you.
   ❖ Cherish its beauty.
   ❖ Revel in the majesty of the sunset, the wonderful aroma of the roses, the delicious taste of good food, the pleasing harmony of music, and the soft touch of a loved one's caress.

3. **Avoid total focus on your goals.** *Never get so caught up in pursuing your goals that you cease to enjoy the present.* **Your life is your journey.** Enjoy what you've got when you've got it. Otherwise,

you might wake up some day and realize that you missed living altogether.

4. **Make the most of each moment.** Realize that every moment of your life is a gift. Get all the good out of it that you can.

    ❖ If you make a mistake, *learn something from that moment* and move on.
    ❖ *Take a cue from your dog.* Have you ever noticed that whatever you do with your dog is his favorite thing? If you take him for a walk, it's as if he thinks, *"Oh boy! My favorite thing!"* If you play fetch, it's, *"Oh boy! My favorite thing!"* When you feed him, it's, *"Oh boy! My favorite thing!"* We could all enjoy feeling more exuberance!
    ❖ *Look for the silver lining.* Practice finding the good, even when things don't go as expected. Many times, you can even get something better than you had planned, if you just open your mind to the possibilities that there is something good to be discovered.
    ❖ *Eliminate time spent waiting.* Avoid just sitting around and waiting for things to happen to you. Take advantage of your time by making it productive. Use it to listen to motivational audio books, share delightful insights with the people next to you, plan your day, or read something that educates, inspires, or relaxes you.

There's a Zimbabwe proverb that says, "If you can walk, you can dance. If you can talk, you can sing." Like the proverb, living in the moment lets you live with excitement instead of mediocrity. Living in the now gives you a reason to dance instead of walk, and sing instead of talk.

Living in the moment takes some practice, but the more you do it, the easier it gets. Practice this every day, and soon it will become a habit that changes your mindset and helps you live a life full of passion, joy, and happiness.

> **"Work like you don't need money,**
> **Love like you've never been hurt,**
> **And dance like no one's watching."**
>
> **~ Irish Proverb**

Choose Conscious Living

Conscious living, just like living in the moment, involves being aware of what's around you and choosing to make the most of what you've got, but it takes things a step further. Conscious living brings in the added factor of making certain choices that can bring you the life you desire.

Conscious living is *living on purpose.* You choose how you want to live your life and then live that way.

Follow these strategies to live consciously and help bring your goals to fruition:

1. **Set priorities in your life.** Decide what's most important to you and live according to these priorities.

    ❖ For example, you're watching TV and your significant other comes in and wants to talk about something that's important to him/her. What do you do?

    Option 1. Do you turn off the TV and listen attentively to him/her? Do you make eye contact and focus on him/her?

Option 2. Or do you let him/her try to compete with the TV, having him/her speak over the TV noise while you multi-task – listening to him/her and watching TV at the same time?

With conscious living, surely your significant other is a priority over the TV, right? Can you imagine how special you'll make him/her feel when you choose to actively and completely listen? *When you live like your relationship is a priority, your relationship benefits greatly.*

❖ *Having clear priorities makes it easier for you to make decisions* about your time, money, and other important matters.

2. **Choose to have an optimistic attitude.** As we've already seen, this conscious living choice can have an enormous impact on your life.

❖ Each morning when you wake up, tell yourself that *this day may be your best day ever!* Helen Keller once said, *"Life is either a daring adventure or nothing."* We don't know ahead of time all the things the day will bring, so look forward to it with anticipation as an exciting adventure and live your day accordingly.

3. **Simplify your lifestyle.** Put the things into your life that you want there, according to your priorities, and eliminate the things that merely serve to clutter it up and cause confusion and stress.

❖ Events and activities that eat up your time and take away from your family time are a good example of things you can eliminate from your life. *Your hectic lifestyle can be a major cause of distractions and stress!* Will it really matter if you decline a couple of parties or miss a PTA meeting here and there? Once you get used to putting only those things in your schedule that you feel are a priority, you'll wonder why you didn't learn to say *no* sooner!

❖ Is your house or office space cluttered? Once again, ***eliminate what you don't want or need.*** Take a weekend to go through everything in your house, organize what you want to keep, and give away what you no longer have a use for.

❖ ***Eat dinner at home with the family.*** Use this time to catch up with each other, share your day, and show support and love. Make this time a priority and you'll soon see some of your family stressors melt away as you build strong relationships that will last a lifetime.

4. **Live according to your principles.** Remember, when you live consciously, you're *choosing* your life. Let your principles guide you in making your priorities and decisions. Above all, get clear on your values, standards, and principles so you can ***be true to yourself.***

Living consciously gives you a chance to start demonstrating the life you desire. You may not have as much money as you'd like, or you might want to lose some weight, or you may be seeking your soul mate, but following these strategies puts everything in motion.

With conscious living, your thought processes are emitting energy harmonious with attracting what you want and your actions are in accordance with them. Rather than spending your time focusing on your lack, you spend your time and energies choosing your life and living it to the fullest, thus attracting more good things in return.

*"Your vision will become clear
only when you look into your heart...
Who looks outside, dreams.
Who looks inside, awakens."*

~ Carl Jung

How Gratitude Can Attract What You Want

Gratitude plays a big part in attracting your dream life. *Feeling thankful for your blessings attracts more things for you to be thankful for!* Even if what you've got isn't much, it can be increased a hundred fold by being thankful for it.

In addition, when you show your gratitude to others for something they've done for you, they're more inclined to do even more. Gratitude strengthens the bonds of friendship and increases the loyalty of business associates.

Here's some food for thought: If you can't feel gratitude for what you've got now, will you ever feel it, or will you just want more?

Follow these tips to show your gratitude on a daily basis and reap the benefits:

1. **Tell others when they make you happy.** The need to feel appreciated is one of our basic human needs. Fulfill that need and share the love! A simple *"Thank you"* can make their day.

    ❖ Your parents and children love to know when they've made you happy. Make it a habit to thank them often.

- ❖ Letting your significant other know how much you appreciate them and all they do will strengthen your relationship. It can also start a cycle of you both doing nice things for each other because you know how much the other one appreciates it!
- ❖ Your friends also like to know that they bring value to your life. Every so often, do something special to show your gratitude.
- ❖ Co-workers, business associates, and clients also like to know they're appreciated. When they do something for you, be sure to say *"Thank you"* and let them know how much it means to you. Offer to reciprocate by helping them when they need it, too.
- ❖ Remember to thank the clerk at the bank, the customer service rep who went out of their way to solve your problem, or the store employee who helped you find what you were looking for.
- ❖ ***The more you make it a point to thank those who make your life better, the more you find to be thankful for.*** After all, you don't want to be taking things for granted!

2. **Keep a gratitude journal.** At the end of each day, reflect on all that is good and write it down in your journal. Reading about all the things you're thankful for can also lift your spirits and motivate you.

3. **When you awake, give thanks for the day ahead** and all its wonderful possibilities. Before you fall asleep at night, give thanks for the day you just had.

Feeling gratitude every day keeps the good things coming. *Nothing's too small to be thankful for.* If you find a penny on the ground, be grateful for the gift. Even if you desire greater wealth, be thankful for the paycheck you just got.

Gratitude helps you feel fulfilled with your life and it sends out energy with those good vibrations!

**"If you want to turn your life around, try thankfulness.
It will change your life mightily."**

~ Gerald Good

Over-Deliver on Your Promises

Another technique that helps you attract the life you desire is to give more than is expected. When you *give* more to others (as opposed to *taking* more), you're sending out energy that attracts good things back to you.

Consistently over-delivering on your promises suggests a mindset of excellence and abundance. Aren't these some of the important qualities included in your dream life?

When you generously give more than you promise, you make others happy. You also feel good about yourself, which strengthens your self-esteem and self-confidence. These are the very traits that you see in anyone who is successful.

So by increasing these qualities and traits within yourself, you're setting yourself up for success in achieving your life's desires.

Use These Mind-Altering Tools to Change Your Life

To transform your mindset into one that attracts what you want, it's necessary to incorporate your desired thoughts into your subconscious. Your mind is like an iceberg, that is, the *conscious* part of your brain is the top 10% and the hidden 90% is your *subconscious*.

It's also your subconscious that controls 90% of your actions and virtually all of your ideas and attitudes that affect everything else in your life. *In essence, it controls you.*

There are some simple strategies that allow you to access your subconscious. The goal is to input the ideas and attitudes you desire into your mind on a continual basis so that gradually your mindset changes to what you want. These strategies allow you to mold yourself to your heart's desire through your subconscious!

Follow these tips to make lasting changes to your subconscious so you can attract your desires:

Positive Attitude. It is all about believing in the idea that your attitude affects your life and what happens to you.

You have to believe in the idea that a positive attitude equals positive results. You have to start looking for proof. It shouldn't be hard to find, since positive influence is all around.

Try it out for yourself. There is no better proof than seeing it firsthand. Take one day and commit to having a positive attitude all day. Take notice of how others react to you.

Here are some samples of maintaining a positive attitude:

- ❖ Upbeat and cheerful
- ❖ Looks at the glass as half full not half empty
- ❖ Can find the beauty in anything
- ❖ Thinks of the good before the bad
- ❖ Loves life
- ❖ Avoids negative words
- ❖ May seem silly at times

- ❖ Loves to have fun
- ❖ Never puts others down
- ❖ Genuinely cares about those around him/her
- ❖ Looks for ways to make others lives better
- ❖ Is a giver, not a taker
- ❖ Does not hurt others
- ❖ Can see the solution over the problem
- ❖ Willing to work towards goals

There are many ways you can begin to shape yourself into a positive person. Take some of your favorite tips below and put them to use in your life to help you become the positive person you strive to be.

Every time you start to find your thoughts drifting to the negative, you have to make a conscious effort to make them positive instead. It helps to train yourself to always find the positive in anything. If you train your thoughts to go to the positive it will go a long way towards keeping a positive attitude.

By maintaining a positive attitude and letting it lead you to good, you are allowing your attitude to become your ally.

Positive self-talk. Your mind engages itself in a conversation – or rather monologue – the entire time you're awake. *Since you spend all day talking to yourself, why not tell yourself things you want to hear?* Keep it positive and good benefits will follow!

- ❖ *Congratulate yourself on every success, no matter how small.* Each success is a victory and leads you toward your goals. Take every opportunity to celebrate and build your confidence!
- ❖ When you make a mistake, ask yourself how this helps you. What can you learn or gain from this error? Even mistakes can bring the very life lessons that can catapult you toward your success.

❖ *Avoid beating yourself up about anything!* This negative self-talk ruins your confidence and breeds discontent and failure. If you hear something negative, stop it in its tracks and turn it into something positive.

❖ Use your self-talk to encourage yourself to act in ways that are in accordance – and not contrary to – your goals.

Affirmations. Affirmations are a form of positive self-talk that affirms the traits in you that you desire. You can replace your negative mindset with positive thoughts and images that guide you toward your goals.

1. *Remember the 3 Ps: Affirmations should be personal, present tense, and positive.* Personal means to use the words "I", "me", and "my". Write them in the present tense as if this is a trait you already possess. And, of course, you want them to be positive statements.

2. *Use them every single day.* Say your affirmations every morning, every night, and whenever you feel the urge during the day and night to boost your attitude.

3. **Here are some affirmations you can start with:**

   ❖ I take advantage of opportunities that present themselves with swift action.
   ❖ I enjoy meeting new people.
   ❖ I am open to new ideas that can help me reach my goals.
   ❖ I take time to plan my actions and then follow my plan.
   ❖ I make healthy choices about the foods I eat.
   ❖ I enjoy exercising because it makes me look good and feel better.

4. **Prayer and meditation.** Take the time to pray and meditate and visualize actually living the life of your dreams. *Experience it*

with all your senses and it will draw it to you. This kind of spiritual self-reflection will help transform your mindset to be in accordance with your visualization.

"Man is made or unmade by himself; in the armory of thought, he forges the weapons by which he destroys himself. He also fashions the tools with which he builds for himself heavenly mansions of joy and strength and peace."

~ James Allen in "As A Man Thinketh"

Living Positive. It's rather simple to separate the positive from the negative. However, it can be quite difficult to stop yourself from running to the negative. This is simple human nature. Don't feel bad about this natural inclination. Instead, choose to do something about it.

Here are some tips for adding some positive influence to your life:

1. **Find a happy place.** Create a place in your mind that is your ideal paradise. When you feel stressed or down just go to your happy place, relax there and enjoy it.

2. **Get a hobby.** Doing something you enjoy and that will raise your spirits and allow you to maintain a positive attitude.

3. **Smile.** Smile and greet everyone you meet warmly. Smiles are contagious, and you'll instantly begin to feel a difference inside yourself.

4. **Be Thankful.** Pause throughout the day to think about things that you are grateful for. The more you practice gratitude, the better you'll feel about life and about yourself.

5. **Exercise.** While many people look at exercise in a negative way, it really can bring positive influences to your life. The body's reaction to exercise is a good one. You will feel better and therefore act better if you adopt an exercise routine.

6. **Exploring new things.** Instead of walking away from the unknown, walk towards it.

7. **Don't walk away from a challenge.** Let yourself accept challenges and try creative ways to deal with them.

8. **Surround yourself with positive people.** Most people who soar to incredible heights of accomplishment in their lives do so because they surround themselves with positive, encouraging people. It's hard to have a positive outlook for yourself when everyone around you is complaining all the time.

9. **Pretend.** The imagination is a wonderful thing. Allow yourself to go to some make believe place. Get away from your normal life and pretend you are someone else. Have fun and you are sure to smile.

10. **Turn a negative into a positive.** Instead of ignoring your negative thoughts and hoping they'll go away, ask yourself if the critic inside of you is trying to teach you something valuable. Take note of the lesson, and then quickly discard the negative thought by replacing it with a positive perspective on the same situation.

You can take these tips and build upon them. Surely you can come up with things that have a way of making you happy. You know what makes you smile, so take that and run with it. Allow whatever it is that makes you happy to guide you to your new positive attitude.

Take Action to Make Your Dreams Come True

If you want anything to happen in your life, you need to take action. When you set a goal, you can't accomplish it without some kind of action. If there's something you are unhappy with, don't put up with it *"just because"* that's the way it is – actually do something about it!

You'll find that when you strive to become action-oriented, more things go your way quicker than ever before.

One reason for this is that taking action keeps you from sitting around just *wishing* for more, while you focus on whatever you're *missing* in your life. After all, if you believe it's missing, then that's just the way it will stay – missing!

Focus, instead, on making a plan and implementing it. As you work to achieve your goals, your focus should be on what you *can* do!

Create an Action Plan You Know You Can Accomplish

Setting yourself up for success with your action plan is important. Otherwise, you might feel as if you're just spinning your wheels. For example, if you set goals that are unreachable, you're quite likely to give up before you ever really get started!

How can you set yourself up for success with your action plan?

Use these tips to set S.M.A.R.T. goals that will bring you the success you desire:

1. **Specific.** State *exactly* what it is you want to accomplish. Rather than saying you want to make more money, state how much more, for example, $12,000 per year.

2. **Measurable.** You must be able to measure your goal so you know when you've accomplished it and can move on to your next goal. The goal in the above example is measurable because it's a *real* number to work towards.

3. **Attainable.** Divide your goal into attainable mini-goals that you can accomplish in a short period of time. If you desire $12,000 more per year, you can divide it into $1,000 per month, or $250 per week.

4. **Reachable.** Is your goal reachable for *you?* Do you have some way you can reach that $250 per week goal?

   ❖ *If not, then rethink your goal.* Perhaps you *first* need to take action on implementing another income stream or you need to go to school to get additional skills or credentials in your current job before you can progress to the $250 per week goal.

5. **Timely.** Set a timeline and a specific date in which all steps will be completed. This will, of course, depend on your goal. If you need to take a 6-month course to further your education or skills, then that first goal will end in 6 months.

Once you're sure you've created a plan you *know* you can accomplish, you've already set yourself up for success. All that's required now is that you follow your plan!

Implementing Your Action Plan

In order to follow through with your plan, there are a few more strategies you can implement to make it a success:

1. **Make the first steps easy and quick.** Put easy tasks at the beginning so you'll be able to jump right in and get started quickly. This will give you confidence and motivate you to keep going.

2. **Reward yourself for each accomplishment.** No matter how small your micro-goals are, pat yourself on the back each time you achieve one of them.

   ❖ Take pride in your achievements and enjoy your success. Remember, this sends out energies that will bring back more things to be proud about!
   ❖ Treat yourself to a little reward for the small goals and a bigger one for completing major milestones. This gives you some immediate gratification and something to look forward to with each step.

3. **Change your plan if necessary.** If you find your plan isn't working for you, it's much better to alter your mini-goals to something that you *can* accomplish than to keep failing at achieving them. Remember, you want to set yourself up for success!

Taking action is a given. Taking the *right* actions can bring your dream life to you a lot faster. This is why it's so important to develop a mindset and attitude that encourages you to take *direct* actions toward success.

A successful mindset combined with an organized plan will complete your bridge to success. All you have to do is take that first step forward on your journey. Once you do, you'll find that the more you give, the more you'll receive. Soon enough, you'll truly delight in the life you always desired!

Signs that Indicate You're Making Progress

Perhaps the biggest sign that you are getting where you want to be in life is that deep feeling of utter contentment and happiness you feel when you get out of bed first thing in the morning, you awake looking forward to a brand new day.

There are many smaller signs that you're going in the right direction towards that which can help you to stick with your plans for change and get you through those periods when you're uncertain or feel like giving in.

Everyone has different reasons for wanting to change themselves for the better, perhaps one wants to lose a few pounds, or stop smoking, etc. One may have challenges with low self-esteem that they need to overcome, or someone may wish to develop better communication skills.

These are just some of the aspects in life that we have to deal with and overcome in order to better ourselves, and of course, as with anything, making any changes to your lifestyle will require some patience.

Noticing changes in yourself won't happen overnight, it could take weeks, even months for you to start feeling the benefits of your changes and seeing those changes, but there are many positive little signs that'll give you encouragement along the way and shows your making progress. Here are just a few of the signs you might see along the way:

- ❖ Every time you look into a mirror, the first thing you do is smile at yourself.
- ❖ You jump out of bed full of energy looking forward to a new day

- ❖ You find you no longer worry whether other people like you are not
- ❖ You do what you want to do instead of what you think others want you to do
- ❖ You get more comments about the big change in you
- ❖ You find the word "no" is in your vocabulary
- ❖ You no longer fear making new friends
- ❖ You actually feel proud of what you have accomplished
- ❖ You can laugh and see the funny side if you make a mistake
- ❖ You automatically learn from your mistakes and shrug them off more easily
- ❖ You are able to reach the goals you set out for yourself more easily
- ❖ You find that you are no longer putting things off, but looking forward to them instead
- ❖ You make changes in your life naturally without even thinking about them
- ❖ You can't remember the last time you had a bad day
- ❖ You just feel you're heading in the right direction

Take these strategies to heart, and live the life you desire - and deserve!

Wellness Tips of the Week

Make it a habit to start to incorporate empowering tools into your daily way of being. Get use to using powerful affirmations. Hang them up in your bedroom, your bathroom, carry them with you on index cards and look at them several times a day. Begin a wellness journal. Be mindful of eating well, getting all the proper nutrition for your body needs. Start an exercise program. The main message here is take care of YOU on the inside and out. Make continuous use of daily success tools for ongoing achievement in your life.

This Week's Empowerment Tools

CHECKLIST

Check everything that you're doing right now, then integrate additional action steps – one at a time – into your everyday routine.

Living In The Moment

- ☐ Watch the movie The Peaceful Warrior.
- ☐ Take time to stop and smell the roses.
- ☐ Avoid total focus on your goals – enjoy your present life, too.
- ☐ Make the most of each moment.
    - ☐ Learn from your mistakes.
    - ☐ Look for the silver lining.
    - ☐ Eliminate time spent waiting.
    - ☐ Feel exuberance and excitement.

Choosing Conscious Living

- ☐ Clarify your principles and live by them.
- ☐ Set priorities in your life and use them to simplify your decisions.
- ☐ Choose an optimistic attitude.
- ☐ Simplify and enrich your lifestyle.
    - ☐ Eliminate clutter from your schedule.
    - ☐ Eliminate clutter from your surroundings.
    - ☐ Eat dinner at home with your family to strengthen your relationships.

Feeling and Showing your Gratitude

- ☐ Tell others when they make you happy.
- ☐ Keep a gratitude journal.
- ☐ Give thanks for your day.

Over-Delivering on your Promises

- ☐ Do I have an abundance mindset?
- ☐ Do I deliver more than expected?

Using Mind-Altering Tools to Change your Life

- ☐ Positive self-talk
  - ☐ Congratulate yourself on your successes.
  - ☐ Avoid beating yourself up about anything.
  - ☐ Find the good in your mistakes.
  - ☐ Encourage your good actions and thoughts.
- ☐ Use affirmations several times a day.
- ☐ Pray or meditate twice daily (in the morning and before bedtime).

Take Action to Make your Dreams Come True

- ☐ Create an action plan you know you can accomplish with S.M.A.R.T. goals.
  - ☐ Specific
  - ☐ Measurable
  - ☐ Attainable - divide your bigger goals up into small goals
  - ☐ Realistic

☐ Timely
☐ Implement your action plan.
    ☐ Start with easy, quick tasks.
    ☐ Reward yourself for each accomplishment.
    ☐ Change your plan if necessary to ensure success.

SELF-REFLECTION WORKSHEET

Use this worksheet to write affirmations that can help you change your mindset, eliminate bad habits, create good habits, and attract the life you desire.

Remember, your affirmations should be Positive, Personal (use the word "I", "me", and "my"), and Present Tense (as if you already exhibit that trait).

You can use affirmations in many areas of your life. I've listed some of the areas you may wish to strengthen below:

Your Financial Life – your career, income, investments, and savings

_____

_____

_____

_____

Your Relationships – with your partner, parents, children, or friends

_____

_____

_____

_____

Physical – eating right, exercising, and good health

_____

_____

_____

_____

Mental Attitudes – your success mindset, confidence, and self-esteem

_____

_____

_____

_____

Your Spiritual Life – your inner peace, faith, and deeper purpose

_____

_____

_____

_____

Habits You Want to Break – addictions like smoking, drinking, over-eating

_____

_____

_____

_____

Good Habits You Want to Encourage – Like exercise, healthy eating, happiness and communication.

_____

_____

_____

_____

Chapter Two: Financial Success Makeover

Quotes to Ponder

The waste of money cures itself for soon there is no more to waste.

~ M.W. Harrison

I am no longer cursed by poverty because I
took possession of my own mind,
and that mind has yielded me every material thing I want,
and much more than I need. But this power
of mind is a universal one,
available to the humblest person as it is to the greatest.

~ Andrew Carnegie

Main Scoop

Financial Success makeover - Strategies to put into action to establish and maintain a successful financial blueprint.

So What exactly Is Money?

There are many ideas of what people think money is.

Some say it is a form of measurement.

A measurement of what? Wealth? In the olden days, people measured wealth by how many cows, sheep and horses they had. How is wealth measured today? All the dollar bills sitting in the bank cannot guarantee a secure meaning of wealth.

Some say it is a form of power.

Yes, money can give you power, but if you are stuck on a desert island forever with a trillion dollars, will that money mean squat to you? If someone offered you water and a helicopter to fly out of there, you would trade all your money in a split second, so money is not an accurate measurement of power – it heavily depends on how and wisely you use it.

Many believe *it is the root of all evil...* and several others take on this belief without much questioning.

Now, now, now... money is **NOT** the root of all evil (*otherwise, religious facilities would not be accepting monetary donations and charity with gratitude and love.*) Now, **The love of money** may be considered the root of all evil. Remember, money is an excellent servant but a terrible master. If you are trading your life away for the dollar, money then has power over your time and life.

And unless you have proper financial intelligence, the lack of money can create a negative mindset as observed in primarily cheats, thieves, criminals, freeloaders, and more to name.

So, what is money, really?

Money is an idea or thought backed by confidence

While money has naturally been developed by merchants in the older days to replace the questionable barter system, money today is literally invented by the wealthy.

Entrepreneurs are willing to part with their money to buy other people's time. Other people's time i.e. *employees and self-employed people* becomes their employer's asset and the employers use this priceless resource to go on to create more wealth for themselves.

And here's the thing: **as long as you work for money, you are enslaved by it! 80% - 90%** of the populations today are being *enslaved* involuntarily.

What many don't realize and should is that there is a part of your soul that cannot be bought at whatever price. Would you chop off your little finger if your boss offered you 24 months of your salary immediately? You and I know we are worth more than that. However, all of us must make a living in order to support our loved ones, and ourselves but the supreme way of doing this is by eventually doing something you love.

On the other hand, we occasionally do hear about someone selling his or her soul for a dollar, very sad thought.

Awareness Before Change

Don't **get me wrong;** I'm not banging on working at a job (I worked at one as well as becoming an Entrepreneur).

But let's face it: our needs today are growing faster than any other period of history. Prices go up, salaries don't. There are more people than ever and they have very little pension to show for their decades and years of work efforts.

And there is no guessing to how many people really, really dis-like the hectic lifestyle they feel they are living, coping with stress for most parts of the day, join traffic jams, spend more money and time in traveling, enjoy very little rest, and repeat the viscous cycle.

Definitely doesn't paint a nice financial and lifestyle picture, huh?

The first step to change is to **be aware of the problem**. Awareness before change is the first step necessary in order to make any changes in life and to start taking control of your financial well-being.

One needs awareness in order to know what state they are in, so they know where it is they are going. For starters, indulge me in a quick exercise.

Time And Money

There are generally 4 types of people in the world:

(1) **No time, and no money.**

Most employees fall into the category. You can't go shopping on a Tuesday afternoon or fire your boss whenever you like. Most employees can't even save money in their pension to last 3 years!

(2) **No time, lots of money.**

Self-employed, professionals and small business owners are in this category. They are slightly better off than the employee because they earn more, but they have to work even harder than employees to keep up with the diminishing profit margins, competition and servicing their customers.

(3) **Have time, no money.**

Many people have lots of time but no money. Maybe ignorance is bliss, but without a stable source of income, how long can you last many days forward?

(4) **Have time, and lots of money.**

This is the category that some business owners, landlords, investors are in. Imagine, not having to work for money, but having money work for you, by investing and earning profits by using your money to make money.

Short Quiz

1. Which one of the four categories are you currently in?

2. Which one category do you desire to be in tomorrow?

Transitioning into a Relaxed Financial State of Being

Knowing how comfortable it feels when you are in a relaxed financial state of being gives you a huge incentive to take a serious look at your own finances. It's very important to develop a successful financial plan that supports a sustainable lifestyle.

Such a lifestyle includes several important features that increase your personal profits:

- ❖ Living below your means – not at or above
- ❖ Learning how to save money
- ❖ Developing additional streams of income

Money is always flowing somewhere, even during financial transitions and challenges. If you develop a mindset that allows you to focus and seek out what you need to do and tweak in order to create more income flow, you will turn all tables in your favor, and you'll do exceptionally well.

This session gives you plenty of ways to become creative and take advantage of the current climate to find your success. When times are challenging you may need to be a little more creative, or work a little harder, but the opportunities are there, just waiting for you to find them!

- ❖ *The important thing is that you take action to bring your desires to fruition.*

The cold, hard reality is that merely reading this session won't increase your income or save you money. You have to take action. When you implement the tips within this session you just might find yourself someday looking back on these times as the beginning of your financial freedom!

Living Below Your Means

Living below your means is the best thing you can do for you and your family. Your personal finances work the same way as those in a business. You always want more money coming in than going out.

What does "living below your means" mean, anyway? When you live below your means, you spend less money than you earn. By no means does this mean that you're living in need, it simply means that you have money left over at the end of the month. This allows you to maintain a positive cash flow that increases your savings and wealth.

On the other hand, when you purchase items with money you don't yet have (such as using a credit card or loan), you're actually living above your means and it costs you more than you may imagine. Consider this:

A $1000 charge on a credit card could take you over 15 years to pay off if you make your minimum payment on time every month. If you pay late or get behind on your payments, it will take you even longer.

When was the last time you acted instead of reacted?

Taking action gives you more control over what happens in your life and relieves stress. Act rather than react! If you thought your mortgage was your only long term debt! Think again, the fact is, the cost of credit is staggering.

When you try to live above your means by spending money you don't have, you end up paying for your money, which sets you behind even further. So make the commitment to live below your means, so you can have some money to spare for your future!

Think about these two questions a moment:

1. What expenses can I cut?
2. What smart investments can I make?

Are you living below your means?

- ❖ Living above your means = Debt
- ❖ Living at your means = Zero savings or "emergency" cash
- ❖ Living below your means = Financial safety and security

Creating a Successful Budget

Creating a budget enables you to choose where you want to spend your money. With a budget, you'll know how much of your money is going where. You'll never find yourself at the end of the month wondering where all your money went, with no way to trace it.

Rather than restricting you, a budget can bring you freedom! It actually frees up income to put you in a better position for financial success. However, the best budget in the world won't help you if you make it too strict, inflexible, or hard to follow.

How can you make your budget successful? Follow these steps to create a budget you can live with:

1. **Determine where your money goes.** Keep track of your expenses for a month or two to see where you're currently spending your income. This information becomes a base for your decisions in creating a budget that closely follows your lifestyle.

2. **Add up your monthly income.** Include money from career, and other streams of income, investments, or any other source that brings in household financial resources.

3. **Add up your monthly expenses.** Be sure to include:

    - ❖ Mortgage or rent, credit cards, loan payments, utilities, and other monthly bills
    - ❖ Transportation, including gas, parking, tolls, public transit, and so on
    - ❖ Regular donations to charities, or other organizations
    - ❖ Groceries
    - ❖ Clothing
    - ❖ Household expenses
    - ❖ Car expenses
    - ❖ Work expenses
    - ❖ Hobby expenses
    - ❖ Education expenses
    - ❖ Emergency fund money
    - ❖ Savings
    - ❖ Entertainment
    - ❖ Any other expenses you have on a regular basis
    - ❖ If you pay something quarterly, divide it by 3. If you pay it yearly, divide it by 12.

4. **Make some decisions.** If your income exceeds your expenses, congratulations! You can now decide what to do with the extra – put it in savings, investments, or whatever. If your expenses exceed your income, take time to figure out a cost-saving plan to make up the shortage.

Do I know where all my money is going, or does it just disappear without a trace?

Putting Your Budget to Work

The cash envelope method is the easiest way to stay on your budget. It allows you to live within your means without having to keep a mental record all the time if you may be exceeding your allotments in any category.

See how easy it is:

1. **Label some envelopes.** First, take a stack of envelopes and label them to match your expenses. Be sure to include envelopes for long term and short term savings, emergency funds, and fun money.
2. **Determine the allotments.** Next, divide your monthly expenses according to how often you get paid. If you get paid every week, divide your expenses by 4. Twice monthly paychecks mean you divide by 2.
3. **Divide your cash.** When you receive your income, divide the cash into the envelopes by putting in the amounts you figured out in the previous step.
4. **Pay your bills when due.** If you pay your bills using cash, great! If you pay the bills by check, put the cash in the bank ahead of time. With this method, you'll always have enough money to pay your bills when due.
5. **Make daily cash envelopes.** The hardest envelope to regulate will be the envelope for the daily expenses. This strategy works: Use a large envelope for the daily expenses allotment, with smaller envelopes inside for each day. If you get paid weekly, put 7 envelopes inside the big one. The money in each of the 7 envelopes is what you can spend for the day. Take the

money for each day from your daily cash envelope. When you run out of cash for that day, stop spending!

6. **Spend wisely.** When you use the cash envelope method, your money is allotted as you get paid. When the money is used up from any one envelope, that's all there is for that category until the next payday.

This method takes some discipline so you don't rob money out of your designated envelopes, but when you get used to it, it becomes a very simple way to stay in your budget and save money. If you find you need to change some portions of your budget, feel free to change it to keep it livable. Just be sure you're not changing it every day according to your whims and what you feel like buying that day.

With very little effort, you'll find your bills being paid on time and your savings growing. When the washing machine breaks or the car needs repairs, lo and behold, you have the cash to pay for life's financial inconveniences!

Even better, you'll also enjoy more fun money and be able to take vacations like never before. Things like that new car or your dream home become achievable. And all this is made possible with the same income you had before, but now it'll be wisely distributed.

See how a budget can set you free? It's not a prison, but a freedom tool! **A livable budget can plant the seeds for your** financial **success and contentment, even during challenging times!** Also be mindful of the importance of knowing your credit score and making sure if it is not already great, to begin taking the steps to ensure it does become great.

2 Wealth Building Models

Everyone wants to make more money, but people are generally split into two categories:

Those who bring results after they are promised wealth first

Or

**Those who bring the results first, then are
rewarded by others afterwards**

Let's explore the two groups in depth.

Those who only move after promised big fat paychecks are more like employees.

<u>There is no right or no wrong with this kind of thinking, but consider: you are once again, trading your precious time for money. Instead of investing your time in an ASSET that generates money, you spend your time working on something that is short term, limited wealth, and does not give you income long after you have stopped working.</u>

Consider also, that this kind of short term vision will only produce limited or temporary results at best. Did you ever see a security guard asleep at work when the employer was not around?

Furthermore, the part where our emotions get the better of us is when we allow our lives to be run by chasing the dollar. It is evident whenever an employee is offered a higher salary, more medical benefits and longer vacations, that their heart starts pumping faster.

A higher salary doesn't mean less financial problems. On the contrary when your income goes up, you're commitments, your tax bracket and your time spent in your company increases, as well as your living expense going up. **The greater your salary, the weaker your position** because if your boss is paying you a 5 figure income and calls for an emergency meeting, *you had better rush over to the office even if you are halfway in the middle of making love.*

Here is one definition of an employee/boss relationship.

An employee will only do the bare minimum to keep the boss from firing them and a boss will only pay the bare minimum to keep an employee from leaving.

Now let's explore the other group.

There are many creative people, inventors, entrepreneurs, and business leaders who fall into this category.

An entrepreneur is someone who always has good ideas.

The first obstacle we need to overcome if we want to succeed in the second group is to **stop working for money**. What does this mean? Isn't making money part and parcel of having good financial IQ?

What I mean by 'stop working for money' is not working for free. Rather, it means work so as to gain the necessary skills you need to be a successful entrepreneur (or inventor, investor). Allow me to illustrate:

If you lack the contacts for running a business, where would the best place be to look for contacts? Of course, your competitor's customers.

How about product knowledge? Then work with a company that will teach you all the ins and outs of the tricks of the trade.

Fear of talking to people? Get a sales job where you will be forced to talk to lots of people. It is also a great way to develop perseverance!

I am sure you heard of the saying that the best education you can get is in real life! Not at a lecture hall.

The bottom-line is: **not everybody has what it takes to succeed as an entrepreneur!**

It is not that easy. Many lack the perseverance, the creative mindset, the financial capabilities or the necessary people to get the job done, and they usually give up too early before any results can be seen! The fastest way to get those skills to succeed is to learn them hands on and you even get paid in the process! Don't get absorbed with how much you are paid.

When Donald Trump was selecting candidates in *The Apprentice*, their first task was to go to the streets and sell lemonade! Many would find it a degrading task. But to The Donald, it was very important: If you can't even do something as simple as sell lemonade, how on earth can you handle a daunting task like running the Trump Empire?

Again, let me emphasize:

Would you trade time for short term money? (Money stops coming in when you stop)

Or

Trade time and money for a long term asset that generates you income? (Even long after you have stopped)

God created us with a brain. All we need to do is look around us and observe problems to overcome because every problem is an opportunity in disguise, and for every negative situation, there is a positive solution.

It is all up to you. You may or may not see the results in the short term, but by using your brains and the resources around, you can create true value that others are willing to pay for.

3 Ways of Making Money

Let me summarize the 3 Ways of Making Money

- Trading Time For Money - employees, self-employed

- Manifesting and Using Creative Ideas - inventors, artists, programmers

- Leveraging on resources and other people - business people, leaders

If you are a professional, have you ever explored writing an e-book about your field of expertise? If well written, it could provide a new income stream, instead of you selling out your time serving your clients.

How about a computer programmer? You can come out with your own revolutionary product instead of selling your ideas to the company you work for.

How about real estate, instead of selling houses, you can pool financial sources to buy houses cheap, increase their value and sell them off at a higher price. It just takes a little time and research to find good ideas.

Is money a problem? Seek out loans if you can take the risk. Pool money from many investors or seek a grant. The sky is the limit when it comes to making money.

Again, which way do you want to achieve wealth? Answer: it's totally up to you

What Does Investing Mean To People? Here is an important little rule about investing.

What comes to your mind when you hear or mention the word investing?

Does it mean, putting your money in insurance, mutual funds, the stock market or even high-yield investments?

Some people may only think about investing when they are about to die and they haven't left anything for their offspring yet.

Some even shiver when they hear the word, often claiming that they have no money to invest or feel that it is too complicated a subject to even discuss.

Many people even invest heavily in health supplements, personal trainers and beauticians to make themselves live longer, become healthier or even look younger! Imagine the advertising budget for beauty companies nowadays.

All these are legitimate concerns when it comes to investing, but I am talking about the most important investment a person can make in his lifetime.

Invest in Yourself

The most important and No.1 rule is "Invest in Yourself" – if you don't, who else will?

Your parents will most likely only invest in your education until you leave college. But that is just the basic necessities provided and does not teach you important lessons about financial education.

Would your boss teach you how to succeed in business so that one day, you will be in his position? Some may, most will not.

You and only you have to be proactive enough to take that responsibility

You see, when you invest in yourself, it means taking on the importance of educating yourself. Education not in the academic or technical sense, though they are necessary skills to be developed in life. Our education doesn't stop at college.

For most working adults, their education enters a stop-stage after they leave college. They stop learning and therefore they stop growing.

We know that IQ is important right? But why aren't the most intelligent people in the world the richest people in the world? Also, there are many accountants and financial planners rushing to their cars every evening trying to beat the after work traffic jams! Why have they not achieved wealth in a way that would sustain a lifestyle of choice, which may not include sitting in traffic jams.

How about EQ or Emotional quotient? Does working hard, having a great attitude and a positive mindset solve ones financial situation? These are important when running a business, let me illustrate:

If you are driving from Boston to New York using the wrong road map, you won't get to your destination no matter how fast you drive your car. You can work harder, but you would only get to the wrong destination faster! You may have the best attitude in the world or the most positive mindset, but you still won't get to New York, although the journey wouldn't bother you as much, since you are feeling positive about it.

You must FIRST invest in your Financial IQ.

Having good financial IQ is not about saving tons of money or dumping them into mutual funds. It is developing a healthy relationship with money and building a wealth of assets that will generate more financial flow.

What does it take to develop your financial IQ? Take a look at the example below

Would you pay for a pint of milk or a cow?

If you buy milk, it is consumed and it is over. You will have to buy milk over and over again when it is finished. Even if the milk costs less than a cow, in the long run, you will still be buying milk again and again.

Now, if a cow were to cost 50 times more than milk, you might pay through your nose when you purchase the cow, but after consuming 50 pints worth of milk from the cow, you would break even on your investment and save more money in the future. In fact, the cow might give birth to 2 or more calves and you could sell one of them for profit!

Get the idea?

EVERYONE is capable of **creating wealth.** When you take a neglected house and give it an overhaul, paint it, fix the roof and change a few minor things that make a big difference in appearance, you could sell that house for more money than if it was just the neglected house it once was. You would have created wealth in the process!

How about a farm? If you turn a farm into a country home getaway resort, wouldn't the value of the farmland increase manifold?

It is the same principle for chefs, computer programmers, artists and craftsmen. The sum of the whole is greater than the parts. We are all capable of creating wealth even out of thin air and that is the first step to getting our creative juices flowing.

The value of anything is defined by **supply and demand**.

You don't need to be a Major in economics to understand this. Money is just an idea. Remember the desert island example? The true measurement of money is not the cents or dollars it represents.

If you have developed a product that people want, would they pay more to you than usual? Would you apply your skills in creating good assets?

<u>Bottom-line</u> is this:

Invest in assets that bring long term value. Anything that brings you more income is an asset. Don't invest too much in liabilities like cars or boats

Homes are not considered assets until they are fully paid off (If you lost your job tomorrow and you can't pay for your house, is your house an asset or liability?)

Are you willing to step out of your comfort zone and pay the price for financial IQ or ignore the signs of the times and expect your employer to take care of you financially for the rest of your life, while never taking risks to better your financial future.

Specific information for the new or soon to be divorced.

Discover the Five Essential Tips for Financial Wellness during your Divorce

Divorce is a major undertaking and transitional time for many. Your emotions are usually running very high during the beginning of your divorce. There are many mixed feelings; you will feel like you are on an emotional roller coaster. You may feel fear, anger, resentment, sadness, shock and many other feelings.

The process of divorce is not easy, and because of this, it is imperative that when you begin, you know exactly where you stand financially. I can assure you that if you have your financial records in order; it will save you many stressful days. You can then use that time more productively; maybe by starting to create a focus on healing, as well as beginning to visualize an extraordinary new start for yourself.

Taking some time to do this will be a major benefit to your overall well-being during this rough road in your life. With that being said, lets move on to the essentials.

Essential Tip One

Get ready, set, start digging through all your financial paperwork. Having all your financial documents in order is a must if you don't want to drive yourself crazy during your divorce phase. Begin by looking for and collecting all copies of important financial papers. The list can be endless. Everyone has a different financial situation, but here is a rundown of some basic information to have on hand:

- ❖ Joint bank Accounts
- ❖ Paycheck Stubs

- ❖ Vehicle Information
- ❖ IRA/401K Plans
- ❖ Tax Returns
- ❖ Loans
- ❖ Insurance-auto, home, life
- ❖ Medical Coverage
- ❖ Credit card Statements
- ❖ Safe Deposit Box Inventory
- ❖ Pension Funds
- ❖ Brokerage Accounts
- ❖ Wills and Trusts
- ❖ Mortgage Statements

It may be worth your time to consult with a Certified Financial Divorce Analyst. As they are specialists in helping their client's to determine exactly what their financial picture looks like, as well as advise what steps to begin taking now to secure a healthy financial future. You may want to take a look at *The Institute of Financial Divorce Analysts,* and *The Academy of Financial Divorce Practitioners.*

You can use the ***Budget Worksheet*** and the ***Money-Saving Checklist*** included with this session, to help you setup your budget and save money.

Essential Tip Two

One of the most important things you must do to make sure you know where you stand with your finances, is to obtain copies of your credit report from the three credit agencies, which are *TransUnion, Experian and Equifax.* You need to know now more than ever what your credit scores are. The main reason for this is that you will be creating a whole new fresh financial beginning for yourself.

You will be walking a new path where you want all roads to lead to success, and having your financial picture right in front of you is a must in order to begin achieving that success. The credit reports will give you a very clear idea of what accounts you hold jointly with your soon to be ex-spouse. It will inform you of any outstanding debts you both may be responsible for. It will give you a good idea of all your outstanding balances that are in both of your names, and your name alone. It will also give you information on any mortgages that you both may be responsible for, as well as any other loans you both may have together or separately.

And most important it will clue you into any delinquencies that may be looming. Sometimes a soon to be ex-spouse will stop making payments on something that they made payments on in the past, they may not inform you of this, and your credit will be affected if you are jointly responsible for that payment.

You should also at this time close all credit card accounts held jointly with your soon to be ex. You can go to http://annualcreditreport.com to get your credit report for no charge.

Get moving on this one, it is a must.

Essential Tip Three

It is very important to start establishing your own credit. While you were married you probably had most of your credit cards, mortgages, and car loans, etc held jointly with your soon to be ex. You may have held some credit cards, mortgages, etc in your own name, which is great, if not start creating this separate credit now by getting a credit card in your own name, use this card on small purchases, and pay in full every month. This little act will help you to build good credit.

Your credit score will play an important role in your ability to obtain new credit, which is why it is so important to know your score. Also your credit score determines what interest rates you will qualify for. One of the best things you can do to give your credit score a swing to the upside, is to pay off any outstanding debts, and also to have good payment history, (paying on time every month). Your credit score can range anywhere from around 300 being the lowest, to 850 being the highest.

If you score is lower than you'd like it, you can apply for a secured credit card. This is where you would put up a certain amount of money, say $700.00 and the issuer will then give you a line of credit for that amount. Make sure that when you get a secured credit card the issuers report to the credit bureaus.

It is also important at this time to get a checking and savings account in your own name.

Essential Tip Four

If you have never been on a budget before, now is the time to take the challenge, and be serious about it; it can only help to empower you towards a strong financial future. It is very important to get a very clear idea of what goes out, and what comes in each month financially. One reason being, that you may need to use this as proof of what standard of living you maintained during your marriage, this sometimes is very useful when determining alimony and child support during your divorce. But more important is that you need to now be able to handle your monthly bills on your own income.

This is a time of adjustment, and right now you need to also adjust financially.

A good way to start creating a budget is to prepare a statement of the family spending. Take a good look at housing costs, utility bills, phone bills (Regular and cell phone). What do you spend on food each month? What extras do you and your family enjoy? Look at your credit card statements, are they easily maintained? Are you able to pay in full each month, or will you be accumulating credit card debt? What will you be bringing in each month financially?

Is that enough to sustain what you are now use to spending? If not tweak it for the time being. You really will not have a true picture until your divorce is settled. Until then get smart, prepare ahead.

If you are a little tight for now, that's okay keep focused on the big picture, you want to avoid financial struggle in the future, and you want to instead prepare for financial wellness. I know the word budget can sometimes bring thoughts of limit to mind, but don't fret, this will actually empower you to begin creating a plan for financial success.

Tap into your network of family and friends for encouragement and support during this time. Read empowering financial books on the subject to spur your creativity on the subject.

Essential Tip Five

Start taking the necessary steps towards building a strong financial plan for your future. Again, during this process of divorce you will be able to start gaining a much clearer picture of your expenses and of your assets; this will be adjusted as you move further towards a settlement. Focus on creating a new financial roadmap for yourself and your family. This is where a good financial planner may come into play.

You can now begin putting your budget plan into action, while also creating financial goals for yourself that you would like to start putting into play immediately. What would you like to financially achieve over the next year? How much money would you like to put towards a savings plan? This is the perfect time to create, and establish these goals, along with taking the steps toward implementing them.

Wishing all the best of success and luck with the transition of this particular situation that some people experience in life.

Here are some things you may want to consider:

- ❖ Updating your will and trusts
- ❖ Create strategies for your IRA/401K Plans
- ❖ Make sure you have the right insurance coverage- home, life, auto
- ❖ Create an asset allocation plan
- ❖ Check into the interest rates on your bank checking and savings accounts
- ❖ Consult with your accountant on the best tax strategies
- ❖ Look at what you are paying in interest on all your lines of credit

If you want to create more income for yourself, or would like a career change to bring in extra money, there are many resources and websites that can help you look into new ways of making extra income, you may also want to start a second part-time job, or start building your own business. Don't forget to fill out your *Income Boosting Worksheet,* included with this session!

Whatever your interests are, go after them with confidence.

So there you have it, the beginning steps towards financial wellness during this temporary stressful phase of divorce. Remember, stay focused, don't rush matters, and do not make any quick moves.

Always take a step back, and look over everything that is presented to you with clear focus. Try not to let your emotions get in the way. Take advantage of local support groups, family and friends.

Keep your head high, and your confidence strong. Empower yourself to survive during this time in your life. Take care of yourself and your loved ones. See your future being great, and it will be.

TIPS ON GETTING OUT OF A FINANCIAL MESS

There are two methods I can recommend for getting out of a financial mess.

Defensive Strategies

The first one is defensive:

Cut down on what you are already spending. You won't have the mindset to start a business while in a financial mess..

Make a list of the things you can and should cut down on. Also, become creative in your thought process, you may want to take away something you do as a luxury temporarily until you are back in good financial standing.

Most important of all, don't buy anything that constitutes a liability. A liability is anything that takes money out of your pocket. Think in terms of cash flow. What can I invest in today that will give me funds tomorrow?

Now let's move on to offensive strategies:

Offensive Strategies

One of the **best, low-cost** ways to invest in your business skills is to join a Network Marketing company, here me out before you pre-judge. As I know, there are many other options, such as starting a traditional business or maybe even an Online Business.

But, If you want to guarantee yourself something concrete where business skills are a concern, my take is on **Network Marketing**.

Regardless of what you have heard about this industry or about the money people may have lost there, the biggest reason why I would recommend everyone to invest in a network marketing company is because of what you can learn there, and not because of how much money you can make (although it would be fantastic if you can make a living out of it).

You see, network marketing companies are the one place where people will share their trade secrets FREELY. It is logical because in order for your upline to succeed, they will want you to succeed as well! Therefore, they will not hold back in teaching you the skills of a business person.

Furthermore, the relatively low cost of investing in a network market-ing company will amaze you for what you can learn for the price you are paying (a few bottles of vitamins and a business kit for the experience of a lifetime!) They will patiently train you in the attitudes and business skills you need to succeed in this industry.

Basically, you can't succeed in network marketing with an employee's mindset. A network marketing company will train you in **sales, communication, teamwork, leadership, positive thinking, self-improvement, time and money investment as well as the support**

of your upline as a personal coach and mentor. I dare say that even if you didn't make a cent, but diligently went through their program, the skills you develop will last a lifetime.

You can also develop skills by attaching yourself to an insurance agency or real estate agency, the jobs may be challenging, but those companies will also teach you the same skills above and you may even gain a few tips on financial planning as well.

How about an Internet business? If you have the aptitude for computers, Internet businesses offer a low cost, high-profit margin business that can earn a lot of money and tap into a worldwide market.

Other places you can learn about business skills can be found at financial planning courses, real estate investment courses, time management courses and lots more.

All these I have suggested will be the safest way you can start a new business. You are only spending a few hundred to a thousand dollars in start-up and education. A traditional business might be too risky for someone without any business experience. You invest tens of thousands of dollars and you might struggle trying to break even. But once you have developed the skills above, you will have a higher chance of succeeding.

The most important thing of all besides a good learning attitude are the people you mix around with.

It has been said before; **you are the sum of the five people you spend the most time with!**

The key point to remember is: **Only mix with Positive thinking people!**

Positive thinking is not wishful thinking. A wishful thinker is a dreamer who doesn't take action. Positive thinking is backed by action and you will feel the energy of people who believe in you and support your dreams.

If you hang out with ducks, you will quack... but if you hang out with eagles, you will soar!

So start looking for people who will follow your vision or are willing to grow together with you.

Lastly, you must **BELIEVE IN YOURSELF!**

The task of stepping out of your comfort zone may seem terrifying and many will not support your dream. They may even go on the offensive even if you don't share your dream.

Then you will be faced with the question, is my financial freedom worth the price I am paying now? Can I live another day with the same routine, the same job, the same paycheck or the same drudgery? If the answer is no, then take action NOW. Not tomorrow, you will wake up and forget about your dream.

Write down your desire on a piece of paper and hang on tight to it everyday. Share it with someone positive and take that first step.

You won't regret it.

My wish is that everyone found this to be helpful. One is always in a transitional state when it comes to finance, and always being aware and not making financial decisions with emotions involved will always keep you one-step ahead.

Wellness Tips of the Week

Learn ways to reduce stress. Stress can be very damaging to your mind, body and spirit. Since it originates in your mind, come up with things you feel you can do to reduce it, and the best results will follow.

Some suggestions:

- Create quite time just for you, learn how to meditate.
- Read a good book
- Exercise
- Get a massage
- Take mini (me) breaks throughout your day
- Be conscious of taking deep, empowering breaths during the day and evening.

Do whatever you need to simply reduce your stress level, that alone will do wonders for you.

This Week's Empowerment Tools

1. Set a goal to create a folder of all your financial records. Make two copies of each financial statement you have. Get two large folders and place one copy of each in the folders. Jot down on the outside of the folder all the paperwork it contains, example--Bank Statement, Credit card statement, etc. In this folder should be everything that was discussed in this session, and anything else you feel is important.

2. Make a list of all your short and long term financial goals.

3. Create a plan of action to implement these goals.

4. When was the last time I tried to follow a budget?

5. Why did I stop?

6. What can I do different this time to ensure success?

BUDGET WORKSHEET

MONTHLY INCOME

Include income from all family members who contribute to your household income.

Paychecks $_____

                                    $_____

                                    $_____

Self Employment $_____

                                    $_____

Investments $_____

                                    $_____

Alimony, Child Support $_____

                                    $_____

Other Income $_____

                                    $_____

Total Income from all sources: $_____

This total should be larger than your monthly expenses. If it isn't, then be sure to implement cost-saving and income boosting techniques to put you into profit!

Monthly Expenses

Mortgage or Rent	$_____	
Utilities: Gas and Electricity	$_____	
Water Bill	$_____	
Phone	$_____	
Cell Phone	$_____	
Internet	$_____	
Cable or Satellite TV	$_____	
Trash Collection	$_____	

Debt Payments:

Car Loans	$_____
Other Loans	$_____
Credit Cards	$_____
	$_____
Savings	$_____
Donations	$_____
Investments	$_____
Other Real Estate	$_____
Groceries	$_____
Gas & Auto Expenses	$_____
Daily Cash (multiply by 30)	$_____
Entertainment	$_____
Clothing	$_____
Household expenses	$_____
Job expenses	$_____
Education expenses	$_____
Emergency Fund	$_____

Insurance:

Life Insurance	$_____
Health Insurance	$_____

TIP: If you pay something quarterly, divide it by 3. If you pay it yearly, divide it by 12 to get the monthly portion of that expense.

Notes and Calculations:

Home Insurance	$_____
Car Insurance	$_____
Other Insurance	$_____
Medical expenses	$_____
Property Taxes	$_____
Other expenses	$_____

Total of All Expenses: $_____

WEEKLY MONEY-SAVING CHECKLIST

Print out a copy each week, post it where you can see it, and give yourself a gold star or a check mark for each money-saving task you do.

	Sun	Mon	Tues	Wed	Thurs	Fri	Sat
Pay yourself first							
Eat at home							
Entertain at home							
Buy in bulk							
Cook extra, freeze							
Brown bag lunch							
Shop with a list							
Use coupons							
Buy on sale							
Comparison shop							
Make your own coffee							
Save your change							
Use cash							
Save gas							
Save electricity							
Use your own cleaning solutions							
Follow budget							

INCOME BOOSTING WORKSHEET

Use this worksheet to reflect on how you can boost your income by tapping into your passions, skills and talents. You will be taken through a series of questions to help you determine the best strategy to create multiple streams of income.

WHAT ARE MY PASSIONS?

_____

_____

_____

_____

WHAT BUSINESS MODEL CAN I USE TO TURN ONE OF MY PASSIONS INTO AN INCOME?

(What services can I provide? What can I sell? Can I create a website? How will I monetize it?)

_____

_____

_____

_____

WHEN DO I PLAN ON STARTING ON MY NEW BUSINESS?

_____

_____

_____

_____

HOW MANY HOURS EACH WEEK DO I PLAN ON DEVOTING TO MY BUSINESS?

_____

_____

_____

_____

WHAT ARE MY START-UP EXPENSES?

_____

_____

_____

_____

WHAT ARE MY INCOME GOALS FOR THIS BUSINESS?

Yearly goal: $_____

Monthly goal: $_____

Weekly goal: $_____

HOW SOON CAN I EXPECT THIS INCOME TO START?

_____

_____

_____

_____

WHAT ACTION STEPS DO I NEED TO TAKE, TODAY, TO REACH MY GOAL?

_____

_____

_____

_____

Chapter Three: Career Blastoff

Quotes to Ponder

Happiness lies in the joy of achievement
and the thrill of creative effort.

~ Franklin Roosevelt

Don't limit yourself. Many people limit themselves to what
they think they can do. You can go as far as your mind lets
you. What you believe, remember, you can achieve.

Mary K. Ash

Main Scoop

Now that you've seen how you can live within your means and save
money, it is a good idea to look into creating multiple streams of
income another source of income can make up for shortfalls in your
budget as well as bring you greater financial security.

In this day and time, job stability is quickly becoming job instability! Never knowing if your job is safe from cutbacks and other issues can be very stressful. The financial cushion provided by additional income can relieve this stress and provide some backup funds if needed.

Creating an income-boosting plan doesn't necessarily mean you need to spend all your free time as a slave at a second job. Luckily, there are many ways to boost your income that can be both enjoyable and profitable.

Even starting your own business is a possibility.

- ❖ Start-up costs can be low.
- ❖ More people are willing to barter their services.
- ❖ You can negotiate lower advertising rates.
- ❖ Many businesses are cutting back on their advertising and customer service costs, thus opening the door to you to turn their customers into your customers instead!

Here are some ideas to set up your own income-boosting plan:

1. Turn your hobby into an income-producer. Set up a website and sell the fruits of your labor to a worldwide market. Start-up costs can be as low as $20 for a website – $10 a year for a domain name and then $10 a month for hosting.

   - ❖ One great thing about selling through websites is that they work for you 24 hours a day, seven days a week, but you don't have to spend all your time there yourself. So you can have money coming in while you sleep, take the day off, or work at your other job.
   - ❖ Do you enjoy arts and crafts? Make things and sell them at flea markets or on the 'net.

❖ Are you a woodworking buff? Advertise your services to businesses or sell what you make directly to consumers.

❖ Do you have an intimate knowledge of golf, tennis, gourmet cooking, or any other popular pastime? Write an informational eBook and sell it on the web.

❖ Set up a blog on the Internet to talk about your hobby. Charge businesses in your niche to advertise on your site and sell your own products for full profits or others' products for a commission. You can also monetize your site with the Google Adsense program, where you get paid when people click on Google ads that are on your site.

❖ Start an informational newsletter about your hobby. You can monetize this by either charging for your newsletter or giving away your newsletter and then emailing product recommendations to your customers.

❖ Set up a paid membership site for fans of your hobby. For example, with gourmet cooking, you can make it a "Scrumptious recipe of the Month" site, following the traditional Book-of-the-Month model.

2. Sell stuff on eBay. Many people make a nice living buying things at wholesale and then selling them on eBay for a profit.

Many wholesalers don't even make you buy the merchandise ahead of time or buy in large quantities. These wholesalers often act as drop shippers, sending the product direct to the customer once you place an order through them. So when your customer pays you, you pay the wholesaler for the product and they ship it out on your behalf.

3. Sell your professional services to others. Do you know graphic design, how to build websites, or programming? Can you write articles or eBooks? These services are in great demand on the

Internet and there are many marketplaces in which you can do business.

- ❖ Do a Google search to find these marketplaces. Searching for "freelance markets" will give you some good results.
- ❖ You can also find customers at WarriorForum.com or Forums.DigitalPoint.com

4. Buy and sell websites. You can also build websites or blogs yourself and sell them to other entrepreneurs on the internet. You can sell these on eBay, Sitepoint.com, or other marketplaces.

5. Buy things at garage sales and sell them at flea markets or on eBay. I once knew a couple who made their living this way and they enjoyed it greatly. In this business, your workdays are the weekends, so it makes a perfect part-time business.

These are just a few of the things you can do to bring in some extra income in your spare time. Most of these ideas don't require much money in the way of start-up costs and you can do them all right from your home.

One of the most important things to remember about starting your own business is to first identify a need that a large group of people have and then come up with a product or service to fill that need. This way, you'll be assured of having a market that's in need of and wanting your product.

Be sure that the need you're filling *is one that people are willing to spend money on to* fill *that need!*

Another important aspect is your unique selling point, or USP. How are you different from your competitors? What more can you offer? Why should someone do business with you? Your USP is important whether you're self-employed or an employee. How can you do the job better than others? What do you uniquely bring to the team? What value can you provide to your employer or customer that few can?

Lastly, develop a lasting, profitable relationship with your customers. Let your customers know you care about them, over-deliver on your product or service, and give outstanding customer support. These qualities are just as important as ever, and they can provide you with a profitable business or career for years to come.

There you have it – how to live within your means, save money, and boost your income. Let this guide give you the confidence to move forward and stronger than ever during any period of your life!

Taking action to follow these tips will show you that you don't have to stress or panic over what's to come. Less financial stress leads to a happier you, healthier relationships, and a more comfortable family environment. If times are challenging for you at the moment, or in transition, or simply not as comfortable financially as you would like it to be, you can thrive if you put a successful plan into place.

Do you have what it takes?

You may have had an idea for starting a business but been hesitant to take the plunge. Building a business from scratch requires skills and determination. I will show you what the basic requirements are that go into starting a business, but before we get started, let's make sure you have what it takes.

There are millions of people who are bursting with ideas for starting a business. However, not enough of them sit down and take a long look at whether they have what it takes to be a successful business owner, or if they need to add some new skills to enhance their chance of succeeding at what they want to begin. Some of the most important characteristics that all business owners need are:

- ❖ **Vision** - You must have the ability to see your goal.
- ❖ **Discipline** - You should be disciplined enough to bear the market's ups and downs, instead of panicking at bad news and gloating at good news.
- ❖ **Curiosity** - You need to want to know how things work or how they could possibly work better to grow your business.
- ❖ **Never-say-quit attitude** - You have the passion to carry through your plans, no matter what the circumstances. You will try to do your very best even in the most challenging situations.
- ❖ **Interest in People** - Finally, it is people who matter the most... Customers who will be buying from you. You'll need to get to know your customers needs in order to be successful.

Now that you know if you have what it takes and you want to start your own business as opposed to working for someone else forever, we'll move on to creating your vision in the form of a business plan. The template is included at the end of this session. Now we'll start with how to put it all together!

Forming Your Business Plan

Go ahead and print out the business plan so we can create a rough draft by taking notes as I walk you through each section. I'm also assuming that you've already decided on what you'll be doing. If you haven't you'll want to do that now, before moving on. You won't need to have any of the planning done; we'll build all that together.

I've also included a list of resources at the end of this session so you'll have a place to turn to while you're planning. I hope it saves you some research time.

Business Summary - You'll want to save pages 3 and 4 for the very end, as they summarize all the planning you'll be doing.

Business Description - Here is where you'll be recording all the details of your business.

Type of Business - Go ahead and jump to page 5 and decide which type of business will suit your needs the best. There is a description for each type of business ownership you can choose from. This will also help you determine where to start when it comes time for licensing your business and how you'll handle your taxes at tax-time. Each location has it's own set of rules so you'll want to research further for your area.

You can find answers to any of your business type or tax questions by visiting the IRS website at: http://www.irs.gov/businesses/small/article/0,,id=99336,00.html

Start-up Costs - You'll want to plan out all the furniture, equipment and supplies you'll need to start your business. Keep in mind that all business start-up requirements are unique, so I've only provided a basic list to get you started.

Once you've determined everything you'll need to get started, it's time to check out pricing. Go ahead and log the budget pricing for now. You can go back later to fill in your actual costs once you start purchasing them. If you already have this item, go ahead an log it with a "0" for the price, since there wont' be any costs associated with it. This will also give you a head start when you fill out your projected monthly expenses when it comes to figuring in the costs of any consumable supplies.

Included in the same section you'll find a place to record the information for your website. All too many times those are left out of the initial planning stages. If they're left out of the planning, your first instinct would be to find free resources so you don't begin spending extra money you hadn't planned on.

Free resources are nice especially when your first starting, but if you can budget for paid services, you'll be much happier as you grow and your needs change.

For example: If you begin using a standard HTML site that's provided for free and you decide later that you want to upgrade to WordPress but your hosting company doesn't have that option you'll be forced to start over from square one. If you find yourself in this situation, you'll end up having to go with another domain, because many times it isn't transferrable, which in turn requires a business rename change. ***Save yourself some time upfront by researching all your options.***

Since you're getting detailed here, don't forget to include your logo, website template, website theme and graphics costs.

Products and Services - Here you'll want to list any products or services you plan on offering. There's also room to record your pricing for each product. We'll get into the individual details further along in your planning process.

Market Research - Record any information that led you to determining your business. There's also room to add any additional research that you haven't done yet.

Customers and Target Market Breakdown - You'll want to record what your ideal customer looks like. I've provided a partial list to get your started, feel free to expand further. You may even add additional information as you learn even more about your customers in the future.

Vision and Mission - You'll want to make sure your vision and mission are clear in your mind, so when you start marketing you'll have most of the work done.

Product Descriptions - Here is where you want to describe your products or services from the customer's point of view. Here's a list of questions to get you started:

- ❖ What are the most important features?
- ❖ What are the most important benefits?
- ❖ What's special about it?
- ❖ What will it do for the customer?
- ❖ What problem will it solve for the customer?
- ❖ How will you deliver?
- ❖ Will you guarantee it?
- ❖ Will you provide refunds?

The more information you can provide up front will make your work easier in the long run.

TIP! When thinking about features and benefits don't forget there's a difference between the two.

- ❖ **Features** - tells about the product.
- ❖ **Benefits** - expresses how the customer feels or gains from purchasing the product.

Competitors - You'll want to take your time with this one. Researching and getting to know your competitors is very beneficial when planning your business. Find 5 competitors and log their URL and a description of their business.

Next you'll want to analyze them individually. Compare them to your business making note of strengths and weaknesses. If you find your plan weaker, build it up until it's stronger. If you find a gap in a competitor business, fill it! Most of all have fun, don't be overly critical as plans can be improved as you go along.

Website - I've included a place to record all your website details as you start setting them up. There is room to record your log in information and passwords so you can keep them all in one place.

Projected Monthly Income and Expenses - You can use this form to project your monthly income and expenses. After you launch your business, you'll want to convert to an accounting program for a more complete picture of your business.

Future Plans - As you start setting things up in your business, you're going to have "ah-ha" moments and this is where you'll record them so you can refer back to them later as you go back to review and update your plans.

Additional Notes - This is just an extra page for you record information that doesn't fit in any of the sections of your plan.

Business Summary - Now you can jump back to pages 3 and 4 of your business plan and fill out the summary portions. As you can see it's much easier with the rest complete.

Now that you're plan is done, you'll want to make sure you go back at least once or twice a year to review and update your business plan. If you have time to do this quarterly, you'll be sure to keep on task and make the updating go much quicker.

Congratulations! The planning really is the hard part; give yourself a pat on the back for a job well done. Treat yourself for this accomplishment and watch yourself smile each time another plan falls into place.

Wise Time Management Tips for Work-at-Home Entrepreneurs:

Time for work-at-home entrepreneurs is their single most valuable asset. Nothing can replace time…valuable, precious time!

No matter how many things are on your 'to-do' list, you still just get twenty-four hours in each day. Sometimes I could use another twenty-four but that isn't going to happen. I'll bet that you could use more hours in your workday, as well.

The thing about those twenty-four allotted hours per day is that we can't spend all of them working. Our families and our friends require some of our time. Relationships must be nurtured; we need private personal time as well, also time to run errands, etc. So, we can allow ourselves just so many work hours each day. Since our working time is limited that means that we must make the very most of the hours that we work. We can't waste time on unimportant details or on tasks that others can do.

When you shave a few minutes here and a few minutes there, you will make more efficient use of your allotted work hours. Here are a few suggestions and in the interest of saving your time (and mine), I'll keep this brief and to the point.

- **Email account efficiency:** We all have various email accounts. We use one account for this and another account for that. Checking each and every email account more than once a day can be a time consuming task that you can very easily make less time consuming by having all of the email that comes to all of your various accounts go to one Gmail account. One email account takes a lot less time than several and you can still maintain all of your various email addresses.

Additionally, you don't need to spend a lot of time reading and answering emails that are not going to add to your bottom line.

Email comes in several varieties. There are emails that are business related, emails that are important but not business related and emails that are simply frivolous and time wasting. If an email has been forwarded several times, don't waste your time.

If an email is addressed to a great many people, don't waste any time on it either. Email can consume a lot of time. You need to filter the important from the irrelevant and only spend time on those emails that are related to your business.

- **Set up timetables to help you prioritize your workday:** A scheduled workday is an efficient work day. You will get a lot more done in a lot less time if you know in advance and can see at a glance what task is next on your list. I like visual aids. A timetable is a visual aid. It can help you allot your time efficiently and productively!

- **Focus on result producing activities:** When you make your work day schedule, you need to be certain that the tasks that you schedule are the ones that will in fact make your business grow and thrive. Don't waste your time, effort and energy on tasks that can be done by others.

Take time to investigate outsourcing. You can add hours to your day each and every day when you outsource the mundane business tasks to others.

You can outsource such tasks as bookkeeping and accounting, article/E-book writing and submission, travel and event planning and ad writing. Others can do these tasks better and more efficiently than you can and your time is better spent on growing your business, making those contacts and closing those deals!

- **Shave time off of counter-productive activities:** Like I said, your friends and families do required some of your time but you can also waste a whole ton of time on such unproductive activities as watching TV.

   You will be really surprised at how much of your day that you waste if you keep a record of your time expenditures over the course of several days' time.

Now don't misunderstand me. We all need down time. We all must relax our minds as well as our bodies. We can't be all business all the time but we can limit our unproductive or counterproductive activities.

Time is precious and time is limited. We need to make the very best use of every minute of every day that we possibly can.

Remember-Time is Always of the Essence

I've heard people say that the main reason that they want to work at home is because they can work only when they want to work. It IS true that you can set your own work hours when you work at home but it does NOT mean that you don't have to have set work hours.

A 'hit or miss' work schedule…or rather, the lack of any work schedule at all, simply will not work. Time is of the Essence! **YOUR time!**

Working at home can be a very, very good thing. You can be at home to see the kids off to school and be at home when they get home. You can put a load of laundry in and it can run through the cycles while you are working.

You can have dinner cooked before a hungry family arrives. All of those things are real perks that you automatically get when you work at home.

Working at home can also be a very, very bad thing if you do not plan your time well and if you do not set up a work schedule that you and your family can live with. When you work at home, time really is of the essence.

You must make very good use of the time that you spend working. If you are not efficient in accomplishing the tasks that must be done, you will either spend too much time working or you will fail miserably at your work at home job or business.

You must set up a work schedule for yourself when you work at home and then you must enforce that work schedule for yourself and insist that you family and friends also adhere to your work schedule.

A job out in the brick and mortar world does two things; **(1) It provides a structure for your day** and **(2) it tells your family and friends that your time is spoken for during your working hours.** You will notice that both of these things that a regular job provides, both relate to your TIME.

Let's discuss the structure that a regular job provides and how you can apply that structure to your work at home job or business. When you have a job that you go to outside your home, you are required to be at that job at a specified time on specified days of the week.

When you have a work at home job or business, you need that same kind of structure. You need to set regular working hours. The freedom that a work at home job provides is that you can choose the hours… but you do have to choose!

Now let's talk about your family and friends and how they are going to view your work at home job. It is a strange but very true fact that your dear mother would not DREAM of calling you at your 'real' job and asking you to drive Aunt Rosie to the beauty salon and wait for her….after all….you are WORKING and can't be expected to leave your job to run errands. Right?

That very same considerate mother WILL call you and ask you to take Aunt Rosie to the beauty salon and wait for her when you are working at home. Why? Because you are at home and available, that's why.

Your dear, sweet mother will not see your work at home job as a 'real' job. Your spouse will also see you as being free to run errands. Your friends will see you as being available for long telephone conversations, lunch or for a coffee catch-up.

You can see the problem. If YOU do not schedule your time and abide by your schedule yourself, others will not. Unless you see your work at home job as a REAL job with REAL working hours, your time will be eaten up. You will not accomplish the tasks that you need to accomplish.

You will fail and find yourself out looking for a REAL job unless you see your work at home job as the REAL THING with regular working hours that make you unavailable for other activities.

The best way to accomplish using your time to your own best advantage with your work at home business is to make a schedule and tell your family and friends what that schedule is.

You don't have to be rude but you do have to be firm. Make it clear to all. *"I will be working between 9 AM and 3 PM Monday through Friday. On those days and during those hours, I am NOT available to run errands or take personal phone calls or entertain company."* Then stick to it!

Learning Promotes Growth in life and in business.

We always have something new to learn. Everyday we play the role of both teacher and student. Being open to learning something new everyday can only enhance the wonderful person you already are. One of the best ways to do this is through reading and listening.

When you are not motivated to begin new projects or to take on new things you should think about increasing your learning. You don't have to be an avid reader and take on novels, but you should read. Reading is good for the brain and it is stimulates the mind. Continuously learning new things will help you to grow as well as becoming more open to take on things you didn't think you could do before, with a grounded feeling of confidence behind you.

Something as simple as reading the newspaper each morning, or at some point during the day or evening, is an easy way to learn something new and stimulate their brain. This is an easy, quick and excellent habit to get into.

Keep in mind, you can read the news online everyday at your computer, as well as choose what it is you would like to read. As a matter-of –fact you can read anything that interests you. Maybe you would like to learn a new skill. You can go to a site that focuses on that skill and read a little bit every day.

Reading is not the only thing you can do to continuously be learning, be mindful that in many daily conversations with others, there is always something new you can teach or learn. Also, if you don't have time to read or if you don't like to read there are other ways you can learn. Many people who have long commutes often listen to audio CD's. Some people learn a different language or listen to a novel. There are many different things you can listen to at any time of day.

Also if you are a television person, you can experiment with different learning channels. You can watch a cooking channel or a financial channel, etc. You don't have to read if you are not a big reader.

Continuous learning is extremely important in any area of your life. Be mindful of learning something new each day through family, friends, newspapers, audio cd's, books, Television, etc. You will be happy you did.

Wellness Tips of the Week

One of the greatest things we have in our control is how we choose to think. When you start getting into the habit of thinking from a positive mental attitude, as opposed to a negative one, you will find that instantaneously you are in a much better place.

Be mindful of shifting the negative thoughts to positive ones. With every-- "oh but" you have, replace it with "I will do."

This Week's Empowerment Tools

Questions to Ponder:

1. What am I going to do to bring in some extra income?

2. Can I schedule in some time this week to take action on making my ideas a reality?

3. What do I enjoy doing?

4. How will I use the income created from this additional source?

Your

Company

Name

BUSINESS PLAN - YEAR

Contents

Business Plan

Business Summary

Business Overview Summary:

_____

_____

_____

_____

Vision and Mission Summary:

_____

_____

_____

_____

Target Market Summary:

_____

_____

_____

_____

Why You?

_____

_____

_____

_____

Product and Service Summary:

_____

_____

_____

_____

Bio Summary:

_____

_____

_____

_____

Elevator Speech:

_____

_____

_____

_____

Business Description

A detailed description of your business.

Type of Business:

- ☐ Sole Proprietor - Most commonly used as a starting point when opening a small business giving you the option to operate under your own name or a DBA - Doing Business As.

- ☐ Partnership - Business shared by two or more people with an extensive business agreement.

- ☐ Corporation - Most formal type of business and is a separate entity from the owner(s).

- ☐ Limited Liability Corporation (LLC) - Owners are referred to as "members" which limits the liability on each of the owners.

Visit: **http://www.irs.gov/businesses/small/article/0,,id=99336,00. html** for more information.

Start-up Costs:

A complete listing of all furniture, equipment and supplies needed to get started.

Office Space:

Item	Budget	Actual
Location:		
Desk		
Chair		
Filing Cabinet		
Totals		

Equipment:

Item	Budget	Actual
Computer		
CD/DVD Burner		
Printer		
Internet Access		
Phone		
Fax		
Headset		
Software		
External Hard Drive		
Totals		

Office Supplies:

Item	Budget	Actual
Printer Paper		
Envelopes		
Stamps		
Pencils, Pens, Highlighters		
File Folders		
Paper clips		
Stapler		
Calendar		
Notepads/Paper		
Planner		
Totals		

Website:

Item	Budget	Actual
Domain		
Hosting		
Autoresponder		
Totals		

Miscellaneous:

Item	Budget	Actual
Totals		

Products and Services

Description	Price

Market Research

Demand:

_____

_____

_____

_____

Trends:

_____

_____

_____

_____

Growth:

_____

_____

_____

Barriers:

_____

_____

_____

_____

Customers and Target Market Breakdown:

Age	
Gender	
Location	
Income Level	
Occupation	
Education	
Business Industry	
Business Location	
Business Size	

Vision and Mission:

Who are you?	
What are you dedicated to?	
What do you provide?	
How will you deliver?	
What makes you/products special?	
Goals?	
How will you measure success?	

Product descriptions (listed in products and services) from customer point of view.

1.
2.
3.
4.
5.
6.
7.
8.
9.
10.
11.
12.
13.
14.
15.
16.
17.
18.
19.
20.
21.
22.
23.
24.
25.
26.
27.
28.

Competitors:

Competitor URL	Description
1.	
2.	
3.	
4.	
5.	

Compare your business to each competitor using the tables below.

Competitor analysis #1:

Feature	Me	Strength	Weakness	Notes
Products				
Price				
Quality				
Service				
Stability				
Expertise				
Reputation				
Location/ URL				
Appearance				
Sales				
Policies				
Advertising				
Graphics				

Competitor analysis #2:

Feature	Me	Strength	Weakness	Notes
Products				
Price				
Quality				
Service				
Stability				
Expertise				
Reputation				
Location/ URL				
Appearance				
Sales				
Policies				
Advertising				
Graphics				

Competitor analysis #3:

Feature	Me	Strength	Weakness	Notes
Products				
Price				
Quality				
Service				
Stability				
Expertise				
Reputation				

Location/ URL				
Appearance				
Sales				
Policies				
Advertising				
Graphics				

Competitor analysis #4:

Feature	Me	Strength	Weakness	Notes
Products				
Price				
Quality				
Service				
Stability				
Expertise				
Reputation				
Location/ URL				
Appearance				
Sales				
Policies				
Advertising				
Graphics				

Competitor analysis #5:

Feature	Me	Strength	Weakness	Notes
Products				
Price				
Quality				
Service				
Stability				
Expertise				
Reputation				
Location/ URL				
Appearance				
Sales				
Policies				
Advertising				
Graphics				

Website

Domain

Purchase Price	
Purchased on	
Purchased from	
Renews on	
Link to Log in	
User Name	
Password	

Hosting

Purchase Price	
Purchased on	
Purchased from	
Renews on	
Link to Log in	
User Name	
Password	

Autoresponder

Purchase Price	
Purchased on	
Purchased from	
Renews on	
Link to Log in	
User Name	
Password	

Merchant Account

Purchase Price	
Purchased on	
Purchased from	
Renews on	
Link to Log in	
User Name	
Password	

Miscellaneous

Purchase Price	
Purchased on	
Purchased from	
Renews on	
Link to Log in	
User Name	
Password	

Projected Monthly Income and Expenses

Income Source	Amount
Total Income	

Expenses	Amount
Total Income	

Future Plans

Add all your future plans here, so you can add them to your plan as you start planning for them.

Additional Notes

Use this page to record any additional information that doesn't fit into the categories above, or other information you'd like to remember.

Chapter Four: Power of Goals

Quotes to Ponder

In absence of clearly defined goals, we become
strangely loyal to performing daily acts of trivia.

~ Author Unknown

"Obstacles are those frightful things you see
when you take your eyes off your goals."

~ Hannah More

Main Scoop

The Power of Goals - Create your goals and shift your life.

"There is one quality which one must possess to win, and that is definiteness of purpose, the knowledge of what one wants, and a burning desire to possess it.

~ Napoleon Hill

Do you find yourself striving to move forward, but feel like you're not getting anywhere?

Take a moment and ask yourself these questions:

1. Exactly how happy are you?
2. Are you ready for a change?
3. Do you love your career or profession?

Every person in the world devotes countless hours to thinking of their future and their present situation in life. Almost everyone wishes that there was something that they could change in their life.

Whether it is *family life, friendships, relationships, career or finances,* everyone wants to change something. The first step to doing that is to set goals. Many of us are great at trying to set goals but most of us have trouble following through with them.

Think about it. How many times have you decided on a course of action and simply didn't follow through with it? That is pretty much the norm for most people.

It may be one of the world's oldest clichés, but patience really is a virtue. Our greatest achievements are accomplished over time, with considerable dedication and perseverance. Neither of those qualities would be possible without patience. The secret to achieving your goals is following through with patience.

To create the right focus and energy towards creating and achieving your goals, consider the facts below.

When setting goals you can:

- ❖ Achieve more in your lifetime
- ❖ Improve your overall performances in life
- ❖ Increase your motivation to achieve the most out of life
- ❖ Increase your pride and satisfaction in your achievements
- ❖ Improve your self-confidence
- ❖ Plan to eliminate attitudes that hold you back and cause unhappiness

When you use goal setting effectively you:

- ❖ Suffer less from stress and anxiety
- ❖ Concentrate and focus better
- ❖ Show more self-confidence
- ❖ Perform better in all areas of life
- ❖ Are happier and more satisfied with life

Goal setting also boosts your self-confidence

By setting goals, and measuring your achievement, you're able to see what you've done and what you're capable of.

The process of achieving goals and seeing your achievement gives you the confidence and a belief in yourself that you need to be able to achieve higher and more difficult goals.

What are the key points to goal setting?

Goal setting is an important method of accomplishing any lifetime achievement. However, there are some key points that you should consider before setting your goals. Let's take a look at what those are.

- ❖ Deciding what is important for you to achieve in your life and making your choices based on this knowledge
- ❖ Separating what is important from what is irrelevant so that your focus is in the right place
- ❖ Motivating yourself towards achievement to ensure accomplishment
- ❖ Building your self-confidence based on the measured achievement of goals
- ❖ Ensuring that your goals are your own and no one else's

You should allow yourself to enjoy the achievement of goals and reward yourself appropriately. You must learn lessons where they're appropriate, and use these lessons in future goals. In learning from mistakes and errors, you are guaranteeing future success.

How Goal Setting Can Go Wrong

Goal setting can go wrong for a number of reasons. When these things happen, it can be devastating to the self-esteem and can make the idea of setting any new goals mute.

Before we can look into what we can do to begin solving our issues with goal setting, let's see what some of the problems can be.

- ❖ Goals can be set unrealistically high. When a goal is perceived to be unreachable, no effort will be made to achieve it. Set realistic goals so that you can best decide how to go about achieving them.
- ❖ Goals can be set so low that you feel no challenge of benefit in achieving the goal. Always set goals that are challenging enough to be worth the effort, but not out of reach
- ❖ Goals can be so vague that they are useless. Be sure to set precise and measurable goals

- ❖ Goal setting can be unsystematic, sporadic and disorganized. Be organized and regular in the way that you use goal setting
- ❖ Too many goals that aren't given priority may be set, leading to a feeling of overload
- ❖ Remember that you deserve time to relax and enjoy being alive and not solely focused on your goals and achievements

By avoiding these problems, and setting goals effectively, you can achieve and maintain a strong forward leap into your future!

Get Motivated To Achieve your Goals

The key to successful goal setting is your ability to motivate yourself and stay motivated until you have achieved your goals.

Getting and staying motivated is not as difficult as it may seem. It just takes discipline. Let's look at the thing that you should do in order to get and stay motivated.

But first, let's take a look at what motivation really is:

- ❖ Motivation is not a product of outside influence; it is a natural product of your desire to achieve something and your belief that you are capable of doing it
- ❖ Positive goals that are geared toward your pleasure are much more powerful motivators than negative ones that are based on fear. The right combination of both is the most powerful and motivating mix.

Now let's look at what you can actually do to motivate yourself:

1. **Visualize the desired outcome.** Create a picture of what the desired outcome will look like, and have this vision in your mind at all times
2. **Create affirmations** to remind yourself of how capable you are at reaching your goals
3. **Watch movies** that motivate you
4. **Listen to music** that motivates you
5. **Find an accountability partner.** Ask a friend or family member to help keep you working towards your goal
6. **Focus on the positive achievements** and not the negatives
7. **Share your successes with others** as this will keep you focused and help you voice your accomplishments

Remember, a little preparation takes you a long way when setting goals. Have fun and celebrate your success!

Everyone has goals. How you follow through with them determines the success or failure of any particular goal.

Some of the most highly successful people have had clearly defined goals that they were determined to achieve. They were creative in their process, and made changes along the way to accomplish what they set out to do. If a circumstance changed, they just tweaked their process, until their end-goal was met. *They know that taking no action is an action to fail.*

It was their choice to succeed.

What is your choice? How serious are you about setting up an action plan to begin achieving your goals? Are you willing to do the work? These are just some questions that would be helpful for you to think about. Becoming clear on what your goals are, deciding what you want, and what steps you will take, as well as how long it will take you to achieve these goals is very important.

Remember it is not about saying you want this or that, or saying you will set a particular goal.

It is about doing the work, going through the process to achieve the goal that counts. That is what will make you successful at attaining what you want in your life.

Hope you are on board to start creating your extraordinary self, with one goal after another being met.

Step One

Simply decide to take action towards setting your goals, and mean it. Understand that goal setting is a powerful tool for personal and professional planning. It is wise to set your goals in order of smallest to largest to be met. As you accomplish each goal, celebrate your achievement, you deserve it.

Begin now by looking deep into yourself, and focus on what you really want to achieve, become clear on the goals you want to work with. See them, feel them being accomplished, and then become the reason it was achieved.

Take a look at all the main areas in your life you would like to work on Career, Relationships, Well-being, etc, and under each one write down the first thoughts that come to your mind under each category:

- ❖ What is important?
- ❖ Where do you want change?

Go ahead start taking the steps to create your best life!!!

Step Two

Now that you have a clear idea of what goals you would like to set for yourself, we can start moving in the direction of setting up an action plan.

Begin by writing your goals down in full description, with timescales next to each of them stating when you would like to accomplish each one. Remember start with the smallest goal first, then work your way up to the largest.

To make this more real and meaningful jot down next to each goal why you want to achieve this goal:

❖ What difference will it make in your life?
❖ How strong is your desire to achieve it?

Asking these questions will help you continue to see why these goals are important to you, and why you should continuously be motivated to accomplishing them.

Go full stream ahead to your success!!!

Step Three

Make a commitment to yourself to prioritize your time. This will help you strategically balance you life better, and you will be in a better position to continuously focus on the important things in your life.

A few days after you write your goals down re-read them, are you still feeling motivated to achieve them? If you are great, if not write better reasons why you want to accomplish the goal, or simply remove it from your goals list. You want to focus on only what is really important to you at this time. It is the reason behind the goal that makes us have a deep desire to achieve it, not only the goal itself.

When you have goals you truly, deep down want to reach, you are more likely to continue to make it a priority to use your time in the most productive way, with emphasis on taking time to consistently, and actively work on that goal each week. You need to put the goal at hand on your weekly schedule. This will now become part of your new success routine. You need to devise a plan of action to reach your goal.

Go ahead; start visualizing all the possibilities, because you are actively working to make them a reality!!!

Step Four

You will find as you go through the process of reaching success with your first goal, that once you do, **your sense of accomplishment will feel great.** This will help you see all the greatness your future holds as you continue to reach one goal after another. You may have an occasional setback, that is normal.

Remember it is how you deal with the obstacles that come your way, that determine whether or not you will succeed with your end result, it is always your choice. It is not the obstacle itself, you can always rise above that. You just have to keep focusing on the end result of success with your goal, and deal with the obstacles as what they are, temporary sidetracks.

Keep moving forward, nothing can stop you now!!!

Step Five

Always break your goals down into sub-goals. Be specific about what day you will work on your goal. What you would like to accomplish that week towards achieving the goal? Being specific will continuously give you clarity and direction, along with keeping you focused, as well as giving you that extra little push you may need from time to time.

Begin getting excited, if you decide to start seriously setting goals for yourself, your life is about to change for the better!!!

So, there you have it. A beginning plan towards helping you to start taking the steps to actively move your life in the direction you want it to go. Now that you will soon have a list of goals you truly want to achieve, always dig deep for your inner confidence to keep moving you forward. **And remember take the smart approach:**

- ❖ **S** - Specific
- ❖ **M** - Measurable
- ❖ **A** - Achievable
- ❖ **R** - Relevant
- ❖ **T** - Time-bound!!!

Goal Setting for Healthy Body, Mind and Spirit

Setting both personal and career goals and reaching them helps you grow as well as making you feel happier, more in charge of your life, and basically a more results oriented individual who is powerful In making their life one in which they love to live. It makes you feel good to set goals and work toward making them happen. Goal setting is simply healthy for your body, healthy for your mind and healthy for your spirit. One of the things to be mindful of when it comes to setting goals is that you do not want to just sit around and talk about the goals you have and what you want to achieve, but you want to write them down and create an action oriented plan of success. Remember, if you just talk with no action, it will create no results and failure, not what you see for yourself.

When you set goals they have to be both realistic and reachable or you will be discouraged if not met within a reasonable timeframe. Always set goals that you can reach with an idea of when you would like to accomplish the task at hand. And create plans of action for other goals that you want to reach, but may take a bit longer and need a bit more planning, training, etc before they come to fruition. It is important to write out your goals and the steps you will take to achieve them. Decide how long it will take you to accomplish each task. It may be in days, weeks, months or even years. Once you do this you will need to set a date that you will begin working toward the goal. Then you can set the project up on a calendar and write down where you should be with each task.

As you begin to set a goal or reach the completion of one, you should track the progress. As you meet certain milestones you should treat yourself to something special because you are one step closer to doing something you feel is important. If you are running behind you might need to pick it up a step, tweak something or extend out the deadline. Be sure that you are only running behind because you underestimated and you are really working according to task.

Goal setting is very important. When you set goals and lay them out with time frames and milestones you will be more motivated to complete them. As you reach certain milestones you will be motivated more than ever to reach the end of the project. This is a very positive way to work on achieving your goals especially if you have had a hard time completing them in the past.

Success takes Planning, Passion and Vision

When you think of creating a plan, it is good to keep in mind that having a clearly defined vision, along with a healthy dose of passion, almost always guarantees success.

There is a lot to be said about the saying *"Begin With the End Result in Mind."* One of the keys to inviting more of what you want in your life is to believe you already have it.

When you create a plan that works for you, along with having the passion to want it to succeed, as well as having the vision of seeing it as your truth, and consciously working towards that vision, it will eventually come to be in some shape or form.

Know where you're going in life. And if you are not sure, take the time to look into yourself and figure it out. If that means hiring a Life Coach, or purchasing a book about self-discovery, then go to it.

The time is now to move towards your future. We cannot get time back, so make the most of your life NOW, be pro-active in how you want your life to play out, it is your show, direct it.

Take the time at some point this week to ask yourself some important questions that will help you get started on your road to self-discovery. I would like to have you think about, and answer for yourself the questions below.

After that I am going to introduce you to a system that I created called "Pro-Active Production" which will further help you to establish, and put into action your personalized success plan.

1. What were you dreams and aspirations while growing up?
2. Name your top three achievements of your life so far?
3. What was special about them?
4. When you are at your happiest in life? What are you doing?
5. Who are the three people that you most admire?
6. Why do you admire them? What characteristics and qualities do they have?

7. If you could do anything you wanted for a living and get paid whatever you wanted, what would that be?
8. What are your greatest strengths? How can you maximize these strengths?
9. Are you consciously aware of, and do you make an effort to help others less fortunate?
10. What pleases you very much in your life right now? What are you not so pleased with?
11. How can you begin to take the steps to make changes with the things that do not please you?
12. If you could pass on one piece of wisdom to the whole world that you have learned to date, what would it be?
13. What do you value most in life?
14. What would you really like to in life? What would really make you happy, fulfill your inner most needs, and make your life shine?

Pro-Active Production System

Action Step One:

Five advantages of having a pristine Goal Setting System:

1. Defined goals-clear vision
2. Better concentration and focus
3. Optimum performance and achievement in all areas of your life
4. Motivation and self-confidence to accomplish what it is you set out to do
5. Elimination of negative attitudes and habits that hold you back

Five steps needed to begin the process of creating a successful plan:

1. Identify and distinguish between long term and short term goals
2. Create a step –by- step action plan for accomplishing your goals
3. Establish direction, set priorities
4. Be in alignment with what it is you want to achieve
5. Use SMART goals—Specific-Measurable-Achievable-Reasonable-Time-oriented

Result- Live the life that is truly in alignment with who you are.

Action Step Two:

Five Advantages of a good time management system:

1. Achieve more
2. Ability to schedule your time more productively
3. Create the perfect amount of professional and personal time for yourself
4. Learn to concentrate on the right things, at the right time, to get the result you want
5. Insight into how your time is spent

Five Steps needed to begin the process of creating a successful plan:

1. Action-develop a strategic focus plan that works for you, and stick with it. Don't fall into the trap of procrastination
2. Prioritize tasks in order of importance
3. Have an organized system in place
4. Create an effective scheduling system for yourself

5. Use tools—daily planner-computer software-books-activity logs-to do lists

Result - Work and Create your life with time tested positive strategies

So there you have it. I hope this process helps to both, spur you towards the direction of your dreams, and empower you to reach for what you want in life.

Remember you can create all that you want; you just have to have the belief that it is yours.

Wellness Tips of the Week

Clear The Cobwebs - Create ways to sift through all that you feel is disorganized in your life.

- ❖ Get a notebook, keep it as you're clearing the path project journal, and begin jotting down everything you want to organize better, clear out of your path, etc.

- ❖ Create a special time each week to check in with this project journal, make it productive, fun and relaxing.

- ❖ Curl up with a cup of tea or hot chocolate and watch how when you become more organized and in control of you life, how you also become happier.

This Week's Empowerment Tools

1. Exactly how happy are you?
2. Are you ready for a change?
3. What are your life goals?
4. How do they affect your daily life?
5. How serious are you about setting up an action plan to begin achieving your goals?
6. Are you willing to do the work?
7. How can you use your goals to get past a current challenge in you life?

Chapter Five: Limiting Belief Buster

Quotes to Ponder

"Fears are educated into us, and can, if we wish, be educated out."
~ Karl Augustus Menninger

"Fear is only as deep as the mind allows."
~ Japanese Proverb

Main Scoop

Are limiting beliefs paralyzing you into passive inaction?

- ❖ Fear of the unknown
- ❖ Fear of failure
- ❖ Fear of change
- ❖ Fear of lack of support
- ❖ Fear of the worst case scenario
- ❖ Fear of success

Look inside yourself. What's really stopping you? Are your fears holding you back? The good news is that you can learn to transform those fears into an unstoppable positive force!

In this session, we'll examine each of these types of fears and look at how they could be affecting you. You'll learn what causes your fears and exactly what you can do about it. You'll also find specific action steps you can take.

Are Your Fears Real?

A wise man once said that FEAR means False Evidence Appearing Real. In fact, the vast majority of our fears never come to pass. Experts have estimated that 90% of our fears are about things that will never happen!

This means we waste an awful lot of time and energy worrying about things that don't matter!

There's a great portion of our life wasted on worrying. There's all the time and energy we spend worrying about things we know we can't do anything about, plus all the wasted effort worrying instead of taking action to overcome solvable problems – but all of this gets us nowhere!

Now back to the question: Are your fears real? Yes. You may fear something that isn't real, but the fear itself is very real and extremely powerful.

Your fear can take the wind out of your sails faster than any challenge. Fear can stop you in your tracks. Fear can suck away your confidence and destroy your hopes and dreams. But fear can be harnessed and transformed into the strongest motivator!

The Fear Effect

Even though fear is felt in your mind, it causes a physical reaction in your body. The "fight or flight" reaction to your fear can:

- ❖ Pump adrenaline into your body
- ❖ Speed up your heartbeat
- ❖ Make your breathing shallow and quick
- ❖ Make you sweat
- ❖ Cause a panic attack

At times, fear can save your life if the danger is real. But in most cases, the danger doesn't exist. It does exist, however, in your mind, so you suffer the consequences of your fear anyway. It can cause anything from stress and anxiety to heart attacks.

Do You Choose Fear?

Can you imagine the great strides you could make if fear weren't an option – if you spent all that time and energy on moving forward toward your goals instead of sitting around worrying about the bumps in the road?

Are you letting fear be an option in your life? How much time do you spend conjuring up doom and gloom with the "What ifs?" You can make the choice to eliminate this self-defeating habit and take action every day to reduce your fears.

You must acknowledge that your fears are real and realize that it's playing havoc with your life every time fear raises its ugly head. As humans, we all have fears of some kind, but we also have the power to change how we allow fear to affect our life.

With purposeful action comes success!

What Causes Your Fear?

Analyzing what caused your fear in the first place can go a long way toward helping you overcome it. After all, somewhere along the way you developed the fear, and then your mind found ways to validate and strengthen it.

Here are some of the most common reasons for your fears:

❖ Childhood experiences. Even experiences you've long since forgotten can be the cause of many fears. Those experiences are still stored in your subconscious and can affect the way you think and feel about current experiences.

For example, if a dog had bitten you as a child, you might be afraid of dogs to this day. Even though many dogs wouldn't hurt a fly, whenever you see another dog your subconscious reminds you to be wary, and these thoughts then further validate the fear.

❖ Perhaps someone called you stupid at school. To this day, even though you may have a high IQ, you feel that you aren't smart and fear that others will think your ideas are silly. Every time you make a mistake, you validate to yourself that you're 'stupid,' which reinforces your fear.

❖ If you're a creative and artistic person who doesn't trust your own instincts, it may be because of one insulting comment a teacher made years prior. It can affect your entire life, even if you know now that the teacher was wrong.

❖ Observations. Many of the things you see and hear about today could be the cause of many fears.

❖ If your brother lost his job and it caused an upheaval in his life, this could be fueling fears within you.

❖ Seeing the failures of others might have ingrained fears into you about never being able to succeed, no matter how much you want it.

❖ In the same way, seeing great success from your friends or colleagues might also stir up fears within you. You might feel the pressure to compete for fear of failure.

❖ Beliefs. Throughout your life, you've learned things from others. Many times these things aren't based on facts and may even prove to be incorrect. They could have been only opinions, but you learned them as truths, and they cause fears that keep you from pursuing your dreams.

❖ For example, you may fear success because you grew up believing that all rich people are greedy snobs. Every time you met a greedy rich person, it validated this belief. Your fear of becoming a greedy snob overcomes your desire for financial freedom.

❖ You might even believe that money is the root of all evil and that you'll be doomed to hell if you have any kind of financial success. Naturally, your fear of eternal damnation will keep you from succeeding.

❖ You may fear having a great relationship with someone because you've seen too many relationships fail, and you don't want to risk it. You believe relationships invariably end up on the rocks.

Your experiences, observations, and learned beliefs are at the root of your fears. If you reflect on your fears, determine what they are, and then trace them back to their beginnings, you can often gain insight as to why they might be holding you back.

Once you've figured this out, you can start the process of overcoming your fears. But you need to figure out what it is you want to overcome before you can do anything about it!

Trace the cause of your fear and change your belief in It. Fears can keep you from achieving your dreams, but after some reflection you can find the fear behind the fear and overcome it.

Once you've found the underlying limiting belief, you can start feeding your mind with new information that builds a fresh mindset. You can validate and strengthen the new beliefs by focusing on things each day that support your success.

Here's how this strategy works, step by step:

- ❖ Write it out. Get out a sheet of paper and something to write with.
- ❖ Start with the obvious. Write down an obvious fear that limits you. We'll use a lack of confidence as an example.
- ❖ The good, the bad, and the ugly. Underneath your fear, list every time your lack of confidence stopped you. Write down the positive outcome that could have occurred had you not stopped yourself. This step helps you make the conscious decision to change.

- ❖ Quote yourself. What was your self-talk in your most unconfident moments? What was going through your mind?
- ❖ Remember. What experiences, observations, or beliefs could have made you feel this way? Write them down. Go back in your memories as far back as you can.
- ❖ Ask yourself, "Why?" Are there additional fears that could be causing the lack of confidence? Find the fears behind the fear.
- ❖ Are you afraid people will think badly of you? Why?
- ❖ Do you fear failure so much that it takes away your confidence? Why?
- ❖ Reflect. Could you have been misinterpreting some of these experiences negatively in order to validate your fear? Are you trying to reinforce your fear or break it apart?
- ❖ Determine the truth. Write down new beliefs based on truth, not fear.

For example, to combat your fear of failure, write down all the times you've succeeded at anything – big or small. Change your focus to success instead of failure.

- ❖ Validate the new belief. Each and every day, notice and congratulate yourself for every success. You'll be building a new pathway in your mind for your success channel. Soon the pathway for the fear of failure will fall into disarray as the one for success is strengthened.
- ❖ Fear is an emotion. Many times you may feel stressed or afraid without really knowing the cause. This strategy will help you find your fears, acknowledge them, then break through your limiting beliefs.

It will force you to develop a new, positive mindset that you can strengthen with each passing day. Eventually, your subconscious will accept the new belief as the truth it seeks to validate.

With this method, you're truly facing your fears without trying to ignore or bury them.

Once you've determined what your fears are and you've started to change your beliefs, there are still more actions you can take to jump-start your new life without fear!

In the next section, we'll look at some specific types of fears that may be holding you back, and give you actionable tips and techniques for overcoming them.

Strategies to Overcome Specific Fears

Fear of the Unknown

Fear of the unknown is one of our greatest fears. When we don't know what's ahead, we often let our wandering mind take over. Our imagination goes wild with one scary "What if" after another.

- ❖ What if he doesn't like me?
- ❖ What if I spend tons of time with my client's, and don't make the sale?
- ❖ What if I get laid off?
- ❖ On the other hand: What if he does like you? What if you do make the sale? What if you do keep your job?
- ❖ Which scenarios do you focus on? If it's the first three, then your fears are in control.

Follow these tips to lessen your fear of the unknown:

- ❖ Know what you want and how you want to get there. When you know what you want, you're anchored and focused. You aren't blown away by the slightest breeze. You act rather than react.

❖ When you get in your car to go somewhere, you can't see the entire route, but you aren't scared to start the car, are you? In the same way, make a plan to achieve your goals and get started on your way. If you have to take detours, so be it!

❖ Be prepared. Planning ahead naturally helps to reduce your fear of the unknown.

❖ Go ahead and allow yourself some "What ifs" and make contingency plans for probable obstacles. The difference here is that you're preparing solutions in advance, not simply worrying about everything bad that can happen. You're making it easier on yourself.

❖ Example #1: Keep an emergency kit in the trunk of your car with a flashlight, flares, tools for minor repairs, and a first aid kit. Do regular maintenance to keep the car running smoothly.

❖ Example #2: Add funds to a savings account regularly so that you have the money to cover emergencies. A good goal to start with is to accumulate an amount equal to 3 months of your household income.

❖ Be flexible. Keep your plans flexible so you can adapt them if need be.

❖ Seek solutions. When challenges arise, devote your time and energy to finding workable solutions, rather than fretting and worrying. Worrying won't get you anywhere.

❖ Nurture your curiosity. When you're curious about something, you feel a sense of excitement. Life is an adventure! Become curious about what adventures lay ahead for you and you'll look forward to whatever may come, rather than dread the worst-case possibilities.

❖ Live in the moment. Yesterday is already done and tomorrow may never come. All you have is the present. Every moment is precious, so make every moment count! When you immerse yourself in the present moment, you don't even think about – or fear – what may be around the corner.

The best example I've ever seen about living in the moment is the movie The Peaceful Warrior. The movie is based on the life of Dan Millman, a world champion athlete. When a tragic accident leaves him paralyzed, a mentor appears who teaches him to live in the moment. Although the doctors say he may never walk again, Dan stuns them all when he uses his philosophy to become a world class athlete once again.

Not only can living in the moment eliminate your fears for the future, but it can also propel you toward a life of happiness!

Fear of Failure

"Where are you? Here. What time is it? Now. What are you? This moment."
– from The Peaceful Warrior

And the best way to have this confidence, as stated earlier, is to set S.M.A.R.T. goals.

What are S.M.A.R.T. goals?

S.M.A.R.T. is an acronym for the ultimate goal setting technique.

Here are the 5 steps for setting S.M.A.R.T. goals:

- ❖ Specific. Avoid generalities. Rather than saying you want to run faster, you can say that you want to be able to run a mile in four minutes flat.

❖ Measurable. You should be able to measure your goal so that you know when you've reached it. If you want to save more money, then put a dollar figure on it. If you want to lose weight, then state how many pounds you want to lose by a specific date.

❖ Attainable. Regardless of how big your goal is, divide it into attainable micro-goals. If you want to lose 20 pounds, then make a monthly goal of losing 5 pounds each month for 4 months. As you reach each smaller goal, you'll be motivated to keep working toward the bigger one.

❖ Realistic. Do some self-reflection here. Are your micro-goals realistic for you? Be honest for the best success!

❖ Timely. Set a timeline for your goal. In doing so, it will keep you focused on achieving each micro-goal, while helping you brush away distractions.

Here's an example of a S.M.A.R.T. goal: I will save $50 per week by depositing the money into a savings account. It meets all the criteria above. If my bigger goal is to save $2,500 in a year, the smaller weekly goals will get me there in 50 weeks. It may seem like a long time, but success is more than possible with a rock-solid plan.

Also, you'll want to be flexible with your goals. If you need to, adapt your plan – there's nothing wrong with that! It's better to make a new plan that will work for you than to worry about failing in your original plan. Your success will reduce your fears and spur you on to completion.

Realize, also, that everyone has some sort of failure in order to really succeed. In reality, the same mistakes you fear might be the one thing that brings about your success. Overcoming challenges often gives you the ideas you need to succeed.

For example, Thomas Edison tried hundreds of times to invent a commercially viable incandescent light bulb. Each failure taught him something that brought him closer to success. How do we remember him? Do we think of his failures on his journey to success, or do we think of his success – the light bulb?

Changing the way you think about failure can help transform your fears into success!

> "I've lost almost 300 games...26 times I've been trusted to take the game winning shot and missed...I've failed over and over and over again in my life...And that is why I succeed."
> ~ Michael Jordan

Another biggie that affects many of us is the fear of change. Does change make you uncomfortable, even if it's a change for the better?

One of the best ways to get more used to change is to initiate changes yourself. Start with small changes in your daily routine.

- ❖ Take a different route to work.
- ❖ Try a new food. You might like it and find a new favorite.
- ❖ Read a book or play a game instead of watching TV.

Think of these small changes as adventures. Little by little, you'll get used to making changes on a regular basis and discover many pleasurable consequences as a result. These good feelings will start to replace your fears.

The idea is to build your tolerance for change. Soon enough, you'll find that you're looking forward to more and varied experiences, and even the big changes will be easier for you to handle without fear!

Fear of Lack of Support

Sometimes you may fear that no one will support you in your pursuit of your goals. This fear may be unfounded or it may have some vestige of truth behind it.

Here are some tips to help you get to the bottom of this fear and take action to stop it:

- ❖ Discuss your feelings with loved ones. The trick here is to first determine why you feel the way you do. Talk to the people that you'd like to support you. Find out the truth – will they support you or not? Let them know what you desire in terms of support.
- ❖ If you get positive feedback, set mutual goals with the other person. By involving your close family and friends with your goal setting, you'll be far more likely to gain the support you desire.
- ❖ If you get negative feedback, ask them why they feel that way. Work out a plan together that eliminates the obstacles holding back their support.
- ❖ Perhaps it's a fear of their own that prevents their support. Work with them on reducing their fear.
- ❖ If the reason is because they think you need to further develop your knowledge or skills first, then take the advice to heart. Are they right? If so, proceed with further education. If not, show them how qualified you are.
- ❖ You have four options: Act on the advice of others, come to a compromise, prove yourself and your qualifications, or find another support network to rely on.
- ❖ When you've put everything out in the open like this, your fears will lessen because you now have the knowledge you need to deal with any lack of support, if it exists.

Fear of the Worst Case Scenario

One of the greatest fears that can paralyze any of us is the biggest "What if" of all: the worst case scenario. However, just as with the fear of the unknown, remember that most of these fears never come to pass.

Take these actions to bring the fear down to a size you can handle:

- ❖ Stack the odds in your favor. Give your project more of a chance to succeed than to fail.
- ❖ Do your research on the best ways to succeed with the project or venture.
- ❖ Further your skills or knowledge before starting the project.
- ❖ Get your support network in place.
- ❖ Set your S.M.A.R.T. goals.
- ❖ Take action on some small, achievable tasks to jump-start your successes in your plan.
- ❖ Be prepared. Make your contingency plan for a quick recovery just in case.
- ❖ Figure out your recovery plan if the worst case scenario does occur. If you fail in a business venture, how long will it take you to regroup and move forward? If you don't get the job, what are you going to do next?
- ❖ Weigh the risk with the reward. Is your reward of a more fulfilling life worth the risk of a few months of hardship if things don't work out?
- ❖ In many cases, you'll discover that the risk is worth the reward.

Once you've stacked the odds in your favor and you've prepared for a quick recovery, you'll feel more secure and you'll be ready to move forward with confidence.

Wellness Tips of the Week

- ❖ Take a bath
- ❖ Take a drive
- ❖ Take a yoga class
- ❖ Anything that can help you to begin clearing your mind of dust that no longer needs to be there.

Get use to truly enjoying your own company. We all need consistent quality time with ourselves in order to check in and see how we are doing from a deep level within us.

When we do this, we can always be ready to tweak changes when needed, focus on goals, enjoy and bring joy into our lives, as well as deal with what is not working for us, and what we would like to change.

This Week's Empowerment Tools

Fear-Crushing Exercises

In addition to the techniques and strategies we've already mentioned, you can do simple daily exercises to grind your fears into dust and take back control of your life. You can reach out for your dreams, or let them wither and die, strangled by the fears within you. It's your choice.

Here are some exercises you can do every day to reduce your fears:

Keep your self-talk positive. All day long, you're involved in a dialog with yourself inside your mind. When a fearful thought presents itself, acknowledge it, then say something positive to yourself. If an image of failure shows up, replace it with an image of success.

Use affirmations. Affirmations are positive statements that you repeat to yourself every day to change negative beliefs into positive ones. You really can change your life with affirmations, one thought at a time.

Make your affirmations positive, present tense, and personal (i.e. use the words "I", "me", and "my") for the best effect.

Here are some good fear-reducing affirmations to get you started:

- ❖ Life is a great adventure and I look forward to what is to come.
- ❖ I plan my work for success and work my plan.
- ❖ I feel courageous and ready to take on the world!
- ❖ I can handle any obstacle with confidence in my pursuit of my dreams.
- ❖ I enjoy each moment to its fullest.

- ❖ I take action every day to reach my goals so I can live the life I desire.
- ❖ Write some of your own affirmations that counteract your personal fears, and then repeat them every time you feel anxious or worried.

Pray and meditate. Prayer and meditation can melt away your stresses, fears, and worries to relax you at the end of your day. On the other hand, it can also energize you and strengthen you for the day ahead. Take advantage of its special qualities to eliminate your fears and bring peace to your life!

A Simple Meditation Technique:

1. Go into a quiet room, close your eyes and clear your mind. A good way to do this is to focus on nothing else except your breathing until your mind quiets down. Take slow, deep breaths.
2. Once your mind has settled, take yourself to your happy place. Imagine a place where everything is good, beautiful, and peaceful. Enjoy just being there in peace.
3. Then visualize all your fears floating away. Think of them as clouds of smoke, dissipating in the gentle breeze. You breathe in courage and purity and breathe out fear.

With your fears gone, think of all the benefits of your life without fear. Imagine yourself having already achieved your dreams with courage and ease.

Feel the positive emotions – the joy and pride of being present in the moment. Let this excite and energize you!

When you meditate every day like this, it's gets easier to master your fears because you're choosing a peaceful heart over a stirred soul.

Release your fears by doing what you love. You can release your fears by journaling, painting, exercising, or engaging in any other activity that helps you to relieve tension and anxiety.

Do what frightens you. You'll never know just how much control your fears have over you until you confront your fears head on. Just do it, even if you're scared. Once you've faced your fear and made it through, you'll feel like you can face anything, and you'll develop a stronger courage, too!

Take this one step at a time. For example, if you fear public speaking, start out by just talking to a stranger. Then, push yourself further and extend your comfort zone little by little.

As you develop courage, you'll often find that other fears dissolve away. In your mind, things won't faze you as easily and, if you can tackle that fear, you have the power to take on anything!

Your dreams are yours for the taking. Your fears are natural, yet you can naturally overcome them!

Use these tips, techniques and strategies to help you conquer your fears. Even implementing just one of these tips each day will give you the courage to persevere further. The most important thing is to take action toward your dreams.

You can choose to take back control of your fears and, soon after, you'll enjoy the very luscious fruits of your labor!

"You gain strength, courage, and confidence by every experience in which you really stop to look fear in the face. You must do the thing which you think you cannot do."

~ Eleanor Roosevel

Chapter Six: Blissful Relationships

It all Begins with YOU!

Quotes to Ponder

"Some of the biggest challenges in relationships come from the fact that most people enter a relationship in order to get something: they're trying to find someone who's going to make them feel good. In reality, the only way a relationship will last is if you see your relationship as a place that you go to give, and not a place that you go to take."

~ Anthony Robbins

"True forgiveness is when you can say, "Thank you for that experience."

~ Oprah Winfrey

Main Scoop

It all begins with you

I cannot stress enough that if you do not love and take care of yourself first, it will be very difficult to authentically love someone else to the best of your ability.

Think about this for a moment, we have all heard the saying a million times before "When you take care of and love yourself first, you will then be better able to take care of, and give your best to the people you care most about". How many of us follow this prescription?

It is very true that when one is confident and secure in their own skin, then relationships either intimate or any other, will be much healthier and happier.

In sticking to intimate relationships for the moment. If you can find a place of confidence and happiness that is real, as well as keep a fulfilling life both separate and together from your lover, along with having interests, both together and separate, then you are one hundred steps ahead towards maintaining and continuing to grow a special, long-term bond of happiness with that special person.

If for some reason you feel you are not as happy or confident a person in relationships, as you would like to be, you have the power to change that, starting now. You have full control over your life and the decisions that you make. There are many factors which people measure happiness and confidence by. Some people think money is happiness however they may be absolutely miserable with what they do on a daily basis to make their money. Others think flaunting tons of jewelry, etc will make them appear confident, not so.

You might look at people who you think have absolutely everything and you strive to be like them. Things such as, what appears to be an amazing relationship with their significant other, wealth, possessions, status, etc. These things don't create happiness, nor do they create confidence. Happiness and confidence are both a choice.

There are many people who have wealth and high status who are completely miserable. Others who have been in long-term relationships, which on the outside appear great, but on the inside, totally not connected or in tune with each other. The people you think have it great, may be lonely, unhappy, and have low self-esteem and more. Happiness comes from within, while Confidence is a true belief in one's powers, abilities, and capacities.

Some people are naturally happy. This is proven through a genetic disposition. This doesn't mean that you were born to be miserable if you are not a naturally happy person. It just means you need to be conscious of making the changes you wish to become a happier person. Your happiness is influenced by your genetics but it is not fixed as a determining factor.

If you are not a naturally happy person you can change the way you think and feel, it is all up to you. You can learn to do things on a daily basis to bring up your happiness level which will help you learn to become a happier person. The simple action of smiling, even if you are feeling a bit sad, will automatically make you feel happier.

If you are not as confident as you would like to be, take the steps now to become more comfortable, happy and satisfied with who you are both inside and out.

The law of attraction to create blissful relationships

Your personal relationships are a vital part of your happiness. You want to make sure that the person you chose to be with on an intimate level is someone who can help bring out the best in you, while you help to bring the best out in them.

It should be a mutually empowering, honest, unique connection, with a very special unity between the both of you, with the goal of always wanting the best for your partner.

You do not want to fill your life with people who bring you down and have a very low level of positive energy. You don't want to constantly be dealing with the drama of someone else's unhappy events and life that they have chosen to live. Yes, people do have down periods, and you can of course be there to support and help them through their time of discomfort, but if it is a regular way of being for them, then you need to re-think the part that you want to play in this unhealthy role. As continued unhappiness and bad drama, arguing, etc can only cause mishap, none of which you want to deal with on a daily basis.

You in fact want to have a partner who wants nothing but everything good for you. Someone who truly cares about your well-being, an honest, loving person. You want a relationship where each of you gives, respects and helps each other and the relationship to be the best for each of you. You want to be able to agree to disagree, argue in a healthy manner, and then let it go. You want to hold no resentments towards each other, not be afraid to share your thoughts and work together for the best in the relationship and in helping each of you to be happy in all areas of your life. Some of which are areas or things that are shared together and some that are done separately. Point is you need to work in unison to support each other. You want to always be mindful of giving each other inspiration and motivation when needed, and a constant stream of love.

Funny, when you are serious about having a good relationship with someone, and you do the work with yourself needed to be able to create happy relationships, then the law of attraction will work on your behalf to grant your wish. I like to think of the law of attraction as a habit or goal in action.

You should be able to have fun with those around you and not be attached to getting a specific person or outcome. When you are looking for someone to share your feeling with and to laugh and love, all you need to do is send that intention out into the universe. It is good to make a list of all the qualities you want in a life partner and all the qualities you do not want, and then simply send it with love, feeling and excitement into the universe, and it will in turn begin doing its work on your behalf.

Always keep in mind that you need to be doing the best for yourself at all times. It is also very good to be in tune with and listen to your inner feelings. When you are listening to your instincts, you will feel more confident in the decisions that you are making. You have to be confident in who you are and what you want in life. Being prepared for life and all that can come your way is important. Figure out what you want and then go for it. Letting the law of attraction help you be more successful in your personal life will be one way to get to where you need to be.

Believe in who you are and what you want in life. There are so many things that you can do to ensure that you are happy with your relationships. If you find yourself in a bad relationship that makes you fe uncomfortable, really take an honest deep look within, to help disco why. Being confident in what you deserve is important. You need to remember that you are valuable and that you deserve the very best. Get out there and make your life just what you want and so much more.

If you are in a relationship, is everything, as you want it to be? If not, what can you do to make changes in the relationship that will help to make it the best it can be? Are there problems that make it hard for you to love the person that you are in the relationship with? If so, what can you do to help the situation? If you cannot help to change an unhealthy relationship, you need to re-think what you will accept in your life, and how you want to live it. Never settle for anything less than what you deserve. You are the only one that is in control of your life and the relationships that you are in. Be aware of how you are living and if you are truly happy, and if not, what can you do to change it?

Remember that you are the only one that can make decisions for yourself. You need to know that you are the one that knows what is best for you. Tap into the law of attraction, and get clear on what you want in your relationships, and act as if you already have it. Begin taking the steps to create what you want in your life. When you are positive all the time and think about the things that you want it is going to give you strength that is needed to make your personal life better and more fulfilled, as well as help you to make good decisions about your personal relationships.

It is important to have healthy blissful relationships, let the law of attraction work on your behalf by inviting it to do so. Be open to doing more research on this concept and bring it into your life on a daily basis.

Believe in Yourself

Finding love is really a quest within yourself more than a quest outside of you. You need to love you first and know that you deserve love!

Know that you deserve to be happy. When you believe in yourself, you open the doors to love. If you feel that you're undeserving of love, then you push it further and further away from you.

Invariably, others will follow your lead in how you treat yourself and treat you the same way. If you treat yourself with love, others will instinctively love you. If you treat yourself with respect, you can command the respect of others. Never accept disrespect or mistreatment from yourself or others!

Lastly, be real. Being yourself, is being true to you. When you act like you're someone you're not, others will, sooner or later, see through the façade. The dishonesty that started out to make you look good will make you look undesirable instead!

In your quest for love, your belief in yourself will draw others to you. You can see this in action all around you. Those who exude self-confidence always attract more attention from the opposite sex. Recognize your strengths and abilities and be proud of who you are!

Put the Past in the Past

It's important to let go of past loves and forgive those who have hurt you, if you do not forgive, then you are really only hurting yourself.

It's very difficult to welcome new love into your life when you're holding onto emotions, pain and guilt from a past relationship.

How can you begin to let go of these unwanted feelings?

Try these techniques:

1. Use affirmations. When you feel a hurtful emotion about the past, replace it with a statement that evokes a positive emotion instead. It's like recording over a tape or CD.

    * For example, if you feel self-conscious because your old partner said you always-blurted things out without thinking, replace that feeling with a healthy affirmation, say something positive about yourself, such as, "I am a valuable and cherished person with many important things to say."

    * Repeat positive statements when you first wake up, throughout the day, and right before you go to sleep. The repetition helps create and strengthen new neural pathways in your mind while the old, negative pathways fall into disarray.

    * Let one of your positive affirmations be that you forgive the one who you feel hurt you. Perhaps, in reflection, you can realize how you learned something very valuable from that experience and you're better off today because of what you learned.

    * Use positive events as they happen to affirm and strengthen your new, positive beliefs.

2. Write in a journal. Writing your thoughts in a journal can help you reflect on what you are thinking, and can then in turn help release negative emotions, while enforcing positive emotions. One good thing about this method is that you can write anything you want and no one will see it except you.

    Visualize. You can visualize your negative emotions as pieces of paper that you let go into the wind and watch them disappear, ever to return.

Once you've released the past and put it where it belongs (in the past), you're free to focus on your present to bring new happiness and love into your life.

Get Clear-What Do You Want?

What do you want in a mate? Do you want someone tall, short, dark hair, light hair, brown eyes, blue eyes, etc? Is a sense of humor important to you? What about kids? When? Are you looking for someone who shares the same faith? Write down a list of everything you want – the more detailed the better.

Knowing and being able to visualize your ideal partner, will help attract this person to you. It is also important to know what qualities and values you would like a life partner to have. Here are some qualities that build great relationships:

- Honesty - Honesty creates an emotional bond that enables you to share your innermost thoughts and feelings.
- Trust – Being able to trust your partner, and to have trust in your relationship is very important. Trusting one another helps to create a special bond of togetherness, and a feeling of being on the same page in a real way. It's important to have this trust so that you can always share your feelings, thoughts, disappointments, fears and ideas without worrying about being judged.
- Loyalty –Having an unspoken trust of loyalty to the person and the relationship is a very important gift to both of you. It also strengthens your emotional bond.
- Communication - Being able to communicate will always lay the foundation for an amazing relationship. And it is very important to have in order for the relationship to sustain it

and to also grow in a healthy way, as well as help get both of you through a temporary rough spot,

- Common interests, as well as maintaining your own interests, is important in an ideal relationship. It is a wonderful thing to be able to be both together and free in your relationship, it is very important to maintain your sense of self, as well as your sense of togetherness.
- Chemistry - Flirting and friendly fun in the beginning stage of a relationship is important. The chemistry is usually there right from the start, in some cases, it may take a bit of time, however it helps to keep it alive and new. You need to always add spice to your togetherness, try new things, do something different to turn each other on, play intimate games, etc. Use your imagination, and love doing so.
- Physical and Mental Attraction - Physical Attractiveness isn't always a relationship breaker, you need to take into consideration the importance of what I call mental attraction as well. It is important to stimulate each other's mind, as well as being attracted to one another on the physical side. I find that sometimes the physical side can grow on you; it is the mental side that really needs a natural connection.

Once you have your list, make this person real to you. Some of the ways you can make them real include:

- Journaling
- Daydreaming
- Meditating

Focus on what you do want, rather than what you don't want. Imagine t vividly as if you already have this love. Feel the joy and other positive notions you get when you're with this person. Use all your senses envision your times together – walking along the beach, cuddled up by the fireplace, going to one of your favorite places with them, and more.

Imagining every last detail and actually feeling the emotions are an important part to making your vision a reality.

Once you've gained clarity, let it go. Think of this person as someone you'd love to be with, but avoid obsessing over it and feeling desperate to get it, as desperation will only attract more feelings of desperation back to you with events that lead to further desperation. Positive emotions, like how much fun this person is, are the type of emotions you want to feel.

Jack Canfield of the Chicken Soup for the Soul series of books attracted the woman of his dreams by putting his order in to the universe! So can you! Just get clear on what you want, put in your order, and let it go. This, along with taking inspired action, will set things in motion for you to welcome the love of your life.

Give Love to Receive It

People most often gravitate toward others who are much like themselves. If you're looking for love, you want to be a loving person yourself in order for other loving people to enjoy being around you.

Consider being the "personification of love:"

- Love others unconditionally.
- Be open to others.
- Be giving.
- Focus on what others want.
- Have a positive outlook on life.

In giving more love, you'll attract more love back to you and find the love you're looking for.

Prepare to Attract True Love Into Your Life

There are also physical actions you can take to help you prepare yourself mentally for sharing your life with another:

1. Make room in your house. Is there room in your house for another person? You may want to do some clearing.

2. Make room in your bed. Instead of sleeping right smack in the middle and taking up the entire bed, move over to one side a bit.

3. Make room in your garage. If you have a double car garage, but only one car fits in, do some cleaning here, also, to make room for someone else's car.

All these things can help your mind get ready for love and in fact – expect it! Instead of pushing love away, you'll be ready to welcome it into your heart and mind.

Take Action

Regardless of the amount of preparation you go through in getting ready to welcome your true love, it still comes down to action to put your dreams into motion. You most likely won't meet the love of your life if you just sit at home. Yes, love can come knocking on your door, but in most cases you must go out to meet it!

However, you may find love in the most unexpected places. Take, for instance, the grocery store. You may be a frequent visitor to this store and never saw anyone whom you were interested in. But once you've opened yourself to receiving love, things can suddenly take a turn for the better. You might just run into your love-to-be on aisle 5, and them bump into him again in aisle 7.

Be open to everyone around you while doing your daily routines. The person standing in line in front of you at the bank might be the one you've been looking for. The person you meet in the park as you're jogging could be the love of your life. You just never know, but once you're open to receiving, you're inviting love in, so let it come in!

Hang out where they're likely to be met!

Go where your interests and hobbies take you. If you like music, go to a concert. If you like books, join a book club, or hang out in the bookstore. If you like skiing, go to a ski resort, etc. Shared interests are great icebreakers and can help your love endure.

What activities, hobbies, or events will they be attending? Sometimes stepping out of your own regular routine will open up a world of possibilities and fun. Also do what interests you as well. You need not always be on the lookout for a date, or the one. Enjoy your free time to be with friends, or with yourself, relax, and have fun. There is a certain amount of giving it to faith, do not EVER appear desperate. You should love your life as it is. Finding your special someone can only enhance, not make your life. Love your life now, as it is.

Maybe your ideal date is hanging out at:

- Amusement Parks - Everyone loves to ride the rides, play the games and eat the food. Who knows, maybe your next date can be found while having fun at one of these great places.
- Art Galleries - If you're interested in art this is a good way to possibly meet someone else that shares your tastes.
- Book Stores - Hang around your favorite section of the store and see if you notice anyone who interests you. If someone does, find a reason to strike up some conversation about the book their looking at.
- Clubs and Organizations - Are there any charities, causes or events that are near and dear to your heart?
- Concerts - Everyone enjoys going to a concert, but don't worry not everyone has a date when they go!
- Conventions, workshops and seminars- Go to one that you have always been meaning to go to, or one that you are very interested in. This may even be a work related one. Have an open mind, enjoy, learn and be adventurous. Pick one and go for it. You just might make new friends and also meet someone who you would be interested in dating
- Flea market or antique shows and shops - If antiques are your thing make a day of it go exploring.
- Friends - Attend parties given by friends, they may even take it upon themselves to invite someone they think you should meet. Also be open to friends setting up blind dates, that can always be fun.
- Fundraisers - Organizations always throw some of the most interesting fundraisers.
- Gym – This is a great place to make new friends, as well as possibly meet someone you are interested in dating. Nothing is more attractive than seeing someone caring about their health and well-being.
- Café or Coffee Shop - Bring your laptop or a good book, and enjoy an hour or two of sipping on coffee or tea while relaxing.

- Mall - This may be fun when the mall is hosting a function, which attracts vendors and others over the course of a weekend or weeklong event.
- Music Stores - This is just like a bookstore except you want to hang out in the area of your favorite music genre.
- Online Venues - There are some reputable online companies who make it super simple to use as a pre-screening process so you'll know if you even click enough to go on that first date.
- Singles clubs - Is there a local singles club that hosts an activity that you enjoy?
- Sporting events - What are your favorite sports? Go with a group of friends and have some fun.

Finding or putting yourself out there to be found doesn't have to be a chore. Get creative and have a little fun. Love often comes to you when you least expect it.

Setting The Stage for Blissful Relationship's

Let's fast forward a bit now. You've been dating someone and you're really clicking but you'd like to take your relationship to the next level.

Understanding and accepting your partner as is

Nobody is perfect but they certainly can be perfect for you if you can accept them for who they are. The key is to agree to disagree sometimes, and respect each other's differences.

Maybe you're new partner has a hobby that you just aren't interested in. It's ok; sometimes it's those very differences that allow you remain individuals while still being a couple.

There may also be what you think are silly little habits your partner may have, that might get on your nerves, that's okay, we all have them. It's how we choose to deal with them that will make a difference. Is it something that you should be bringing up in a conversation for a possible change or is it truly something that is minor and doesn't need to be addressed? Is it something that will matter to you in 20 years? If it isn't let it go.

How to argue Fair

Every normal and healthy relationship will have its occasional disagreement. When you find yourself in a disagreement, begin first with asking if it will matter in the long run. When you've decided that it's a topic that you both feel strongly about and end up in an argument, here's some pointers to arguing fair.

When expressing yourself in an argument, always use "I" instead of "You" statements. The first time you use "you" in a disagreement your partner is immediately on the defensive side because it makes them feel as if they're being attacked. Instead tell them how you feel by beginning with an "I" statement and they'll be much more open to listening and hearing what you're saying.

There is no winner or loser in a disagreement if you both compromise. Begin with your side of the compromise and what you're willing to give. You'll be showing that you're willing to make adjustments and your partner will be more open to doing the same in return.

When your partner is expressing a feeling that you weren't aware of, follow up by reflecting on what they've just said. For example: "What you're saying is...." This reinforces that fact that you heard what your partner was saying.

When you both can't quite come to terms with the subject, agree to give it a rest so that you both have time to reflect on the conversation. Agree on a timeframe for when you'll readdress the issue at hand.

Do keep in mind that lingering resentment and not expressing your views can build up and create an unhealthy distance between the both of you. So stay on top of resolving what bothers you, and either accept it, and decide it is not that important to potentially ruin the relationship, or work out an agreement. Do not let resentment build it can really hurt a relationship beyond repair.

Praising and appreciating your partner

You've heard the expression that a little can go a long way, and there's no exception when it comes to showing your appreciation. Learning how to express your gratitude will enable you to enjoy improved communication and more fulfilling relationships.

While a grand gesture is always nice and has a time and place, simple gestures are habits that you can add to your everyday routine. It's important not to keep all of your love and appreciation stuck inside your head. Instead, let it out and you'll give meaning, purpose, and joy to everyone around you!

Here's some simple ways to show your appreciation:

- If you think of a compliment that is of course sincere, give the compliment. It's simple and it works.
- Give a card out of the blue. Cards are good for any occasion but the best time to use them is for no other reason than to show your appreciation.

- Go out of your way. Take a moment to think of something simple you can do each day, and every once in awhile maybe something that is above and beyond.
- Bring more hugs and kisses into the relationship. Chances are everyone could use more of "I love you" in their lives, as well as a great big hug.
- A favorite treat might just brighten someone's day!
- Make it a habit to always thank your partner for anything they've done for you, even for simple things like holding the door.

Creating a stress-free atmosphere

More often than not, we tend to focus on too many things every day, leading to confusion, anxiety, and annoyance. This stress can be hard on relationships, but the good news is that you can take measures to lower your stress levels and calm your mind. This will help you to feel better each day.

You can let stress go and feel good every day.

Try these strategies to lower your stress:

1. Focus on what matters to you. What's important in your life? Be proactive about your goals and priorities. When you're working toward something that you want, it makes you feel good about yourself and your future. And when it is incorporated with a goals list, the stress level is reduced, and the productivity level is increased.

2. Find both physical and mental ways to release your stress. Regular exercise, meditation, walking can do wonders for

lowering your stress level. Releasing your stress every day keeps it from building up inside you. Make the conscious choice to start each day fresh, without the stress from the day before.

3. Take quick moments throughout the day to be still, take a deep breath, and then put a smile on your face. Practice these strategies consistently. Work on releasing your stress every day, even on days when you don't feel as much stress, pamper yourself, even if just for a moment. When you're feeling good, it's natural to forget about letting stress go, but it's important to avoid getting complacent and to always be mindful of doing things on a regular basis that relieves stress.

If you practice these strategies each day, it won't be long before you start to feel calmer, even in situations where you would have previously been over the edge. Your thoughts will be clearer, instead of jumbled and racing. Physically, you'll feel stronger too, because your body will be free from stress and anxiety.

Power Partners, Intimacy in top form

Many times we may take for granted the person who is most close to us, our intimate partner. We treat colleague's employees, friend's, and acquaintances with all due respect, and sometimes take for granted the person who is most caring of our heart, and our well-being.

Many times this is not done intentionally; it is just that one tends to feel most relaxed and comfortable with their partner, that they feel safe letting their guard down. That is fabulous, it is only when you start becoming lazy with the needs of nurturing the relationship, ar you start taking advantage of the other's kindness and caring that may run into trouble. When you stop hearing and caring about your partner's needs and wants, trouble can then begin to surface.

It is easy for this to happen, as life can get very busy, and it is often those closest to us that feel it the most, they are also most likely short-changed when we are pressed or rushed with work-related chores, or other things that may be taking our time. Also, if one partner is going through a change of routine, or a life change, it is easy for lack of communication and disagreements to begin surfacing in the relationship.

If you don't nib these issues in the bud early on, resentment then begins to grow, until it escalates into a very unhappy existence between the two, who in the past had the capacity to grow a very strong, loving, empowering connection. One that would help each of you to become power partner's together and separately, one that would nurture, care and create a lasting relationship based on the foundation of love, trust and deep caring for the other person's happiness and success in life.

Working together is extremely important in order for your relationship to deepen and grow. If you work with your partner when each of you are in your separate life transitions and change and grow together, while always keeping the trust, and the doors of communicating open, you will then help the relationship develop into the strong one it has the potential to become.

The problem is, that most of the time in the mist of our busyness, we forget to nurture and care for the relationship, as well as push it's needs aside. By the time we are aware of the damage done, it may be to late.

So what steps can you take to prevent this from happening? Or, possibly reversing the damage, if the relationship was strong enough. The easiest and simplest way, is to always remember to not take your relationship for granted. With that being said, let's look at some other steps that can help.

1- Love--Always remember that love is not enough to keep a relationship strong, and moving full stream ahead. It takes work for a thriving relationship, as well as the commitment of the two people involved.

2- Respect--You need to have respect for your partner. You need to hear what they say. You do not always have to agree, but you do need to respect their thoughts, ideas and viewpoints. You cannot change anyone, nor should you want to. It will not work if that is the case.

3- Trust--This is most important. There needs to be a basic foundation of trust towards each other in order to feel comfortable showing your true colors, as well as expressing what needs to be expressed. You should not have to worry that they will leave if they don't agree with something. If something needs to be addressed and worked out in the relationship, you should feel comfortable with having the knowledge and a level of trust with your partner, that if anything is ever really wrong in the relationship, you have an agreement with your partner that they will come to you to express it, not to other's. It is important to know that any major decisions about the wellbeing, or not, of your union will be made together, just as the relationship was started together. You will want to know that your partner respects and cares for you enough to make all-important decisions about the relationship with you, not behind your back. Sometimes one partner may seeks advice, comfort, etc in someone outside the relationship, unfortunately this harms the relationship, as the other person is not in the relationship and cannot possibly know all the intimacies, issues, etc in it

4- Communication—What can I say, this is a given. You car possibly have a healthy relationship without good, ope honest communication from both sides. This also means hearing and caring about what your partner is saying, and if you don't agree with it, you work on a solution together, you don't leave the conversation forever without making any changes to the issue of disagreement that was at hand. Sometimes one partner may say, let's talk about this another time, yes you can, if you both really set a time and talk about it and then work towards a solution. If a partner says this to move away from the issue, without really wanting to come to a workable, or at least an agreement, it is detrimental to the relationship. You simply cannot survive if one partner does not care to work on an issue at hand. You don't have to agree to do something you don't want to, but you cannot skirt around an issue, and never come to an agreement. If you do this, you are only setting the relationship up for failure.

5- Adaptability- Hey, life and people constantly change. You need to change both together and separately, while having the power to keep your togetherness strong and thriving.

6- Strength- You need to be able to grow and face the fears and challenges and roadblocks that come into any relationship from time to time. Have the courage and faith and love to get through things together, it can only make you stronger. I am not talking here of something that is a major threat to your life, however no relationship runs smooth forever. To have the foundation to get through the tough times together is what makes the relationship something to cherish.

7- Take the time no matter how busy each of you are to connect to each other, share your joy and share your worry. That is one of the best things about being in a healthy relationship; you always have your partner, who you love, trust and can share things with. Hopefully someone that will not judge just be there for you when you need him or her to be.

Wellness Tips of the Week

❖ Spend time by yourself doing something you enjoy.
❖ If you don't already have one, begin writing in a journal that is only for your eyes. Create, express and empower yourself with thoughts and ideas that are by you, and for you.

This Week's Empowerment Tools

Questions to ponder towards opening yourself up to a better way of loving and being loved. After taking your time to answer each one, write on a piece of paper how you envision your relationship with your significant other being. Who are they? What do they look like? What do you laugh about? Begin thinking, visualizing, creating and living in the moment, NOW.

Readiness:

1. Am I ready to include someone else in my life?

2. Am I ready to date someone new?

3. Am I over my ex?

4. Am I expecting a partner to magically appear?

5. Am I positive and upbeat about dating again?

6. Am I happy with who I am?

7. Have I learned from past mistakes?

8. Am I willing to compromise in my next relationship?

Preparation:

Do I deserve love and happiness? Why?

2. How do I treat myself?

3. How do others treat me?

4. Do I have negative emotions from past loves? What are they?

5. What physical traits do I want in a partner?

6. What characteristics do I want in a partner?

7. Do I actively envision my life with this partner?

8. How can I become more open and loving towards others?

9. What are my hobbies and interests? What is my partners?

10. Where does my future partner hang out?

Partnership:

1. Do I accept my partner as is?

2. Will this silly habit matter in 20 years?

3. Do I use "I" instead of "you" when in a disagreement?

4. Do I say "so what you're saying is..." to show I understand?

5. Are we actively working on love?

6. Do we respect each other?

7. Do we trust each other?

8. Do we communicate?

9. Do I show appreciation for my partner?

Remember the importance of loving your life as is and loving yourself first. After this, you will then be open to welcoming another into your life as a romantic partner.

Chapter Seven: Inner Image Magnificence

Quotes to Ponder

"Don't wait until everything is just right. It will never be perfect. There will always be challenges, obstacles and less than perfect conditions. So what. Get started now. With each step you take, you will grow stronger and stronger, more and more skilled, more and more self-confident and more and more successful."

~ Mark Victor Hansen

Once we believe in ourselves, we can risk curiosity, wonder, spontaneous delight, or any experience that reveals the human spirit."

~ E. E. Cummings

Main Scoop

Let Your Inner Essence Shine

The best you is a happy and confident you. Be mindful that if there are things in your life that you would like to change or make better, you are the only one who can create a plan of action and implement it. If you are not happy with the way your life is, or how a certain situation is working out, it is up to you to change it. Too many times, people wait for others to come in and make the changes that they want in life instead of making the changes on their own. It is not up to someone else to create change in your life, it is up to you to do that. It is not difficult to change your life if that is sincerely what your intention is. You just have to realize what you want to change and fix and then take steps towards making that change a reality.

The first thing that you need to do is discover all the wonderful amazing things about you and your inner essence. You are such a unique person with special gifts and qualities that are yours alone, become familiar with them and learn to truly appreciate and love all the gifts you were blessed with. If you think negatively about yourself, stop and concentrate on the positive aspects of your personality. Do not focus on your physical appearance, as this is not as important as you think it is when it comes to confidence, loving yourself and uniqueness. Also remember, with the physical you have a vast amount of people attracted to different things. Focus instead on what is truly important, and that is who you are as a person. You have probably noticed people who were very attractive but who did not come off as someone who you wish to get to know. You have probably also noticed those who are not as attractive as others and who tend to draw people to them. Physical Attractiveness is different for everyone, sincere inner beauty is something all appreciate and cherish.

A case in point. I had a friend in college, who I will call Eric. Eric really liked me and wanted to date, I however, was very attracted to this guy, who I will call David. Many girls were crazy about David, and so when he asked me out, I was very happy. We dated a short time, and during that time Eric and I were still friends, and enjoyed each other's company at different times during the day, when I would see him between classes.

A funny thing happened, I got to know both David and Eric. It wasn't long before I realized that Eric was the person I wanted to get to know better. David had zero personality and was very conceited to say the least, as well as fake beyond belief. You can say he was all fluff. Eric, on the other hand, was authentic, funny, and great to talk to with no fluff attached. He had a dynamite personality, and turned out to be far more attractive to me than David.

Many people are so wrapped up with the way that they look that they put their personality on hold. They are so self-conscious of how they appear to others that they concentrate exclusively on how they look as if having good looks will automatically draw people to them. While it is important that you look as nice as you can for your own self-confidence, good looks only go so far. Having a positive personality and letting the inner you out of your shell is far more effective when it comes to creating fulfilling relationships of all kinds. No one can afford to just rely on his or her looks alone.

In order to discover the best inner you, you have to let go of the outer you and stop letting your appearance speak for you. This is not to say that you totally let your appearance go and do not pay attention to how you look, but that you do not rely on your appearance to do all of your talking for you. You need to focus on your inner essence and begin to let it naturally shine.

Keep in mind, all of us have aspects to our personality that are pleasing and some that are not so pleasing. You will want to accent the positive and minimize the negative when you let the inner you come out. You can make a list of your positive personality attributes as well as those that you see as shortcomings. Then you can take a look at your shortcomings and see how you can turn them into a positive, or minimize them so that they do not compromise your personality, you can also begin to take the necessary steps towards changing things within yourself that you are not pleased with.

You should also realize that the negative components of your personality do not account for your entire personality. They are just components and many of them can be changed. If you have a quick temper, for example, this can be seen as a negative component of your personality. It is better that you do not have so quick a temper in order to put your best foot forward. You may want to try some exercises at controlling your temper if you feel that it can get in the way of you allowing your inner essence to shine through.

There are most likely many aspects about your personality that you really like. This is what you need to capitalize on when you are allowing your inner self to shine through. Make up a list of these positive attributes and see how you can use them to your advantage, while at the same time taking steps to change or minimize what you are not crazy about.

Let's take a quick look at sensitivity, which often is seen as a weakness, when it really is a strength. You can use this strength in a way that will allow your inner self to come through by realizing everyone has an area of sensitivity in their personality. Also focusing on helping others who are less fortunate than you can boost your self-confidence level.

If you have an artistic soul, make sure that you let this out as well. You will want to share your artistic expressions with everyone, as well as those who are likely to appreciate it. You should not be afraid to let your creative nature out and should move in circles where there are other creative people if this is a strong suit of your personality.

Take a look at what interests you and see where your interests lie. Then try to gravitate towards others who share these interests. This will give you a sense of self-confidence and will also help you define your personality.

You should not be afraid to let your inner self shine and release itself. Those who are hampered by fear of letting their true self out in the open become a virtual prisoner of that fear. No matter who you are, no matter where your interests lay, you can find others who also share these interests and who will accept you for who you are.

Letting others sneak a peek into your true self can be very scary for some people. This is why it is a good idea to start with a group of like-minded individuals. You are more likely to get acceptance from this group and can then move on to others. Once you are not afraid to allow your true self to be exposed to the world, your confidence level will naturally soar.

Do not allow your appearance to dictate who you are to others. Take control of your personality and be the person that you envision your-self to be, not just a person in the mirror. Freud had a theory of who we really are that stated that, we are how others envision and imagi us to be. This is an accurate statement about our inner selves and also means that we have the ability to control not only how others see us, but also how we see ourselves.

What is considered to be good self-confidence?

When you are confident in your ability to trust yourself, love yourself and make good decisions based on your wants and needs, I would say that you have a healthy level of self-confidence.

Of course one always wants to be mindful of being respectful and caring of other people. You do however need to be able to do what is best for you at all times. In this way, you are not only better able to be there for others in a meaningful way, but you will also be better able to achieve more of what you want, all the while giving your best to others you care about.

You would also more likely be able to accept and learn from constructive criticism in a healthy way. You will know that you do not know it all, and there is always something new to learn, and you look forward to it enthusiastically.

You will also not be affected by other people who may have negative energy or jealousy towards you. You will be aware that, that is their issue not yours. You would be able to sincerely wish them the best, and move forward without skipping a beat.

What is low self-confidence?

You probably know that low self-confidence is the amount of value you see in yourself. If you see yourself as having little value your confidence if likely low. Also, if you define yourself by the way others think of you, that is far from healthy.

We all may face periods of low self-confidence in our lives at one time or another; it is how quickly we bounce back that matters most. The good news is it can be fixed quickly and with a little work, as long as you really want the change.

Why is low confidence so detrimental?

Low self-confidence can leave us believing that we aren't as valuable as others or that our needs are not as important. Have you ever felt this way?

If so, be reminded that such a belief can create problems in your life, and the belief should be changed the moment it is thought of, as well as the moment you feel your confidence slipping, you should immediately change your thought process to the positive.

Being in a mode of low self- confidence pretty much determines the overall quality of your life at that moment in time.

Why is this so?

It all comes down to your beliefs about your worthiness and value as a person. If you don't believe you're valuable and deserving of good things, you'll push them away.

❖ You'll shy away from healthy relationships with others
❖ You'll avoid setting and achieving goals
❖ You won't strive for a better way of being, thinking you're not worthy of it.

I could go on and on, but I'm sure you're already aware of all the ways low confidence levels can limit many areas of your life.

Have you given any thought to the ways low confidence levels may have prevented you form creating a truly satisfying life? Even if you're relatively happy, know that a boost in confidence can make life even more enjoyable and meaningful!

How did you get here?

Many people have no clue how they may have ended up with the low level of self-confi dence they may have at any moment in time. Sometimes people who were abused in some way or neglected tend to have more challenged unhealthy self-confidence levels.

Luckily, it is relatively simple to re-train yourself to believe in the wonderful person that you truly are. And also that whatever may have happened, had nothing to do with you, if you did not agree to, but were subject to certain things out of your control. You're thought process can and will change, you already took the first step by reading this book. And you can see why and how you may have low confidence levels.

But what if you didn't have an abusive or traumatic childhood?

Most often, it's the result of negative comments and attitudes by the important people in your life. They usually don't intend to be cruel or hurtful. Most of the time they intend to be helpful by offering criticism or guidance, but their words sink into your mind and ultimately shape the way you feel about yourself.

Here are a few more examples:

- ❖ If your parents were very busy and distracted when you were growing up, you may not have received the attention you craved. Their actions may have made you feel like you didn't matter. They didn't set out to make you feel that way but it's your interpretation that left you feeling that way.
- ❖ If your parents gave you attention only for the "bad" things you did, you internalized the things they said. If they didn't balance out the negative with positive message of praise, you'd likely begin to see yourself in a negative light.
- ❖ If you were picked on by other kids in school for being "different" than they were in some way, you may have eventually started to believe what they've said, even if it were not true.

There are many possible examples but all of them have one thing in common: "Someone said negative things to or about you and you internalized them enough to believe them to be true."

I'd also like to point out most of the time they don't set out to make you feel this way. In the end it doesn't really matter what others did or said, it's what you choose to do about it now that'll repair how you feel about yourself.

Regardless of what they did or didn't do...it's up to YOU!

Do your best to identify and challenge those negative beliefs. Ask yourself if you're willing to believe that they were not true after all. You don't have to do anything about them yet, just begin shifting your thoughts about them.

In order to turn these beliefs around, you need to challenge them and be willing to believe something else.

This process of examining and challenging your beliefs will begin to strengthen you from the inside out. You'll stop living your life on autopilot and begin to make more conscious choices in your life. You'll begin hoping and daring to believe that you CAN improve your life, no matter what someone else may have said or did to you in the past.

What's the first step?

Stop speaking negatively to or about yourself as much as possible. If you catch yourself...stop and turn it around with more positive comments.

Example: Let's say that you just said, "I can't believe I just did that, I'm so stupid sometimes!" Stop yourself in your tracks and say, "Wait a minute. I'm not stupid just because I made a mistake. Everyone makes mistakes. I'll learn from this one and do better next time."

The exact words don't matter, except that you gradually stop abusing yourself with hurtful comments.

Remember that this is a process and you won't turn it around in one day.

Learning to treat yourself kindly

How would you treat someone else you cared about? Not only would you not abuse them, you'd probably also do nice things for them, wouldn't you?

You'd also probably:

- ❖ Tell them you cared about them

- ❖ Buy nice things for them from time to time
- ❖ Encourage them when they needed encouragement
- ❖ Do whatever it took to make sure they felt loved and cared for

Now it's time to start doing these things for yourself too!

Do things you enjoy

People with low confidence levels often avoid doing things they enjoy because they're either so busy trying to please others that they don't have time, or they've simply lost touch with that part of themselves.

From now on, start making time to do things you love, such as:

- ❖ Engage in creative pursuits
- ❖ Socialize with friends and loved ones
- ❖ Read books and watch movies
- ❖ Spend time journaling your hopes and dreams

Just have some fun!

Treat your body like a temple

One common result of low confidence levels is that people tend to neglect themselves and end up feeling less than their best. Don't do that to yourself! Give yourself the care and attention you deserve - even if you're not quite sure you deserve it yet.

- ❖ Get enough rest
- ❖ Exercise frequently
- ❖ Eat nutritious foods

Be good to your body!

Treat yourself

Not only should you take care of your body and have fun but you should give yourself treats! They don't have to be expensive treats, just something that'll bring a smile to your face. Things like:

- ❖ A new journal
- ❖ A new outfit
- ❖ Lunch with a friend
- ❖ A movie

These may seem like small things, but it's often the small things that matter most! Over time, these little actions can make a huge difference in how you feel about yourself, which is the whole point.

A Different Take on Failure

Learn why you should look forward to failure, and how it can help you ultimately get where you want to go.

"There is no such thing as failure"

When you read the quote above, what's your reaction?

Do you think the glass is half-empty or half-full?

What if I told you that only you have the power to decide whether or not something is indeed, a "failure?"

In fact, there are some individuals—highly successful people—who believe the very word "failure" has no place in our vocabulary.

How can you acknowledge your success, even as you utter the word "failure"? Well, you can point out:

a. Everything that was learned in the process of getting to where you are now—was a valuable gift because it taught you everything you need to know up until this point.
b. If you failed at something and it did not go according to plan, or you did not achieve the desired outcome (i.e. "failed"), that in itself is a positive outcome, because now you can make adjustments, become creative, come up with ideas that will work, and learn from any mistake you may have made.
c. If you failed, you know the specific path you took this go round, clearly wasn't the right one and so it has successfully been eliminated and will not be repeated
d. You now are aware of what to do differently in the future
e. The experience has enabled you to grow in some way

"Failure" is feedback

"Failure" can simply be a great way to get us to pause in the midst of our process, and get some critical information to indicate that we may need to change direction, try something new, continue our learning, or shift our focus.

Imagine what would happen if we didn't get that feedback, and continued endlessly along the wrong path, toward the wrong goal, or without ever learning a new approach?

The thought of that is pretty scary, isn't it?

Failure should really be seen as positive feedback—information that can get us back on the right track!

Without it, we would not have the necessary clues to success.

The key then, is to identify what is not working or what has failed and change direction, try something new, come up with a new creative approach or shift your focus.

Here are some tips:

- ❖ Always have a clear idea of where you want to go and continue to re-evaluate it as you move forward

- ❖ Identify specific milestones or markers along the way, to let you know you're on the right track and celebrate each success

- ❖ If something doesn't appear to be working, or working fast enough, don't hesitate to try something new

- ❖ Continually learn—from others with whom you work, seek out experts, find others who may have traveled down a similar road before

And always remember:

"You may have a fresh start any moment you choose, for this thing we call "failure" is not the falling down, but the staying down"

"You NEVER fail until you stop trying" "Failing is Winning"

De-clutter your life and improve your magnificence

A lot of people carry around with them a lot of "baggage" or "clutter" in their minds.

When I say this I mean that they are still holding onto things that they say they should or should not do, or one person who had a disagreement with another, really wants to talk with the other person, but their pride is holding them back, therefore creating levels of stress deep inside, that is not needed. This is really silly and ineffective, especially if both people want to reach out to each other, and are not doing so because of ego. And, lets not forget all the coulds and shoulds in your life that may also be holding you back – you need to let go of all of this in order to be productive and in positive flow.

Many of us seem to get tangled up in a lot of emotional baggage that takes up tons of time and energy, all the while that time and energy could be put to much better use by focusing on something much more productive.

Are you like this at times?

If you are, check out the inner image magnificence releaser below.

Inner Image Magnificence Releaser

Take a look at your life and get rid of the baggage you do not need, by asking yourself a series of questions and by completing the following exercise.

In effect, what we are doing is making certain tasks "complete", drawing a line under them and moving on.

Another term for this is "psychological completion" or just "completion"

The following set of questions can be taken at one sitting or over a number of hours/days.

By writing the answers down they become more formal.

Get to it and watch your inner image magnificence soar!

1. Putting up with!

   ❖ Make a list of 10 things that you are putting up with at home
   ❖ Make a list of 10 things that you are putting up with at work
   ❖ Make a list of 10 things that you are putting up with in any other area of your life
   ❖ Make an action plan to get rid of/communicate these things that you have been putting up with

2. Unfinished matters!

   ❖ Make a list of things that are unresolved/unfinished in your life
   ❖ Make an action plan of how to reduce this number!
   ❖ Do you need to clear the air with anyone? If so, just do it! Life is too short!
   ❖ Did you ever say that you were going to call someone or keep in touch with someone yet have done nothing about it? If yes, call them or send an email to them today
   ❖ Let go of as many coulds, woulds, shoulds, maybe, oughts as you can. Write these down.

3. Your standards!

- ❖ Write down a list of standards that you are going to have in your life from this day forward. Standards that you always wanted to incorporate into your way of being, but never did.
- ❖ List 5 people who you admire the most. Identify their greatest qualities, behaviour and how they lead their life. What standards do they have? What standards could you raise starting today that would be similar and to your liking?
- ❖ Respect that other's standards will be different from your own. Think of 5 close family members, colleagues or friends – what are their standards and how are they different to yours?

By completing these exercises you will be able to focus more on the here and now, as well as the future.

You will now be able to let go of many of the things that have been taking up your valuable time and attention.

All those things that put a dull shine on your magnificence can now be swept away.

Inner Image Magnificence Magic

Your confidence increases *exponentially* the more you nurture it. It's as simple as removing all sources of negativity and replacing it with confidence-building activities.

When you face your fears, You become *the* expert, you develop your inner strengths, and you nurture your body, your resolve is intensified and your success multiplies.

Review the checklist below to work on the various areas of your self-confidence.

Facing Your Fear

- ❖ Make a firm commitment to face your fear head-on.
- ❖ Take it one step at a time.
- ❖ If self-doubt creeps in, immediately take swift action to counter-act it.

Gain Confidence By Becoming The Expert

- ❖ Gain an intimate understanding of your passions, strengths, and skills.
- ❖ Acquire unique knowledge and insights that no one else has.
- ❖ Ask questions and listen actively to the answers.
- ❖ Educate yourself constantly.
- ❖ Model yourself after your mentor or role model.
- ❖ Accept compliments graciously.

Developing Your Inner Strengths

- ❖ Write down your positive qualities, skills, and talents.
- ❖ Develop a winning attitude.
- ❖ Release past mistakes and replace them with positive life lessons.
- ❖ Visualize yourself succeeding.
- ❖ Pray or meditate at least twice a day.
- ❖ Use affirmations throughout your day.

Nurturing Your Body, Mind, and Soul

- ❖ Know and respect your morals, beliefs, and values.

- ❖ Eat a healthy diet full of raw fruits and vegetables, as well as the appropriate protein levels.
- ❖ Exercise 3-4 times a week.
- ❖ Celebrate what is unique about you.
- ❖ Compare yourself to no one.
- ❖ Be your own advocate.

Inner Image Confidence-Boosting Exercises

These exercises are things you can do every day to overcome your mental obstacles and build your self-confidence. *The payoff for investing a little time in yourself each day is a lifetime of success and happiness!* Are you up to the challenge?

1. **Set yourself up for success.** Make a plan and take action every day to accomplish your goals.

   - ❖ *Divide your goals into mini-goals* that you know you can achieve in a short time. Achieving these small goals will make you proud of yourself and keep you on track toward your big plans. This momentum not only brings you closer to success, but builds confidence, too!

2. **Meditate.** Build your confidence with meditation. By visualizing the achievement of your goals as if it has already happened, you'll sense a great boost in your confidence.

3. **Have a positive mindset.** Be like *"The Little Engine That Could."* The little engine in this children's book said one thing and then acted on it. He said, *"I think I can, I think I can, I think I can..."* Then he saved the day when the big engines with bad attitudes couldn't do it.

4. **Use affirmations.** Affirmations can build your confidence, one thought at a time. Use them every day for the best effect and then again whenever self-doubt tries to creep in.

5. Affirmations are positive sayings of attributes you wish to develop and affirm in your life. They should be positive, personal, and in the present tense.

Here are some affirmations you can repeat to boost your confidence:

- ❖ I am courageous.

- ❖ I can overcome any challenge.

- ❖ I am well-prepared for any situation.

- ❖ I take time every day for myself, and am better off because of it.

As you can see, these exercises take very little of your time, but used consistently, they work wonders on your self-confidence. Strive to include them into your every day routines and feel your confidence soar.

Confidence in Dating

Did you ever see the Austin Powers movie where he lost his *mojo?* His confidence was crushed! In the end he found out that *mojo* isn't something external that can be kept in a jar, but that he had it all along! His sexy and confident aura came from inside and nobody can take that away.

"Yeah, baby!"

Sophia Loren once said, *"Sex appeal is fifty percent what you've got and fifty percent what people think you've got."* Where do you think that other 50% comes from? *It's your confidence, of course!*

Isn't it wonderful when you have a healthy, loving relationship with someone? We all aspire to this goal. Our dreams of a fantastic life always include that special someone we can share it with.

The key to finding such a relationship is found within. In order for someone else to love you, you need to love yourself!

Building your confidence when it comes to dating starts with believing in yourself. When you have this confidence, you gain the natural ability to draw others toward you and develop lasting and loving relationships!

With this being said, there are still a few things to remember that will both build your confidence and strengthen your relationships:

1. **Be honest.** Being honest with yourself and others makes everything so much easier. When you meet someone new, they can often tell if you're making things up, that's why the truth always trumps lies. *You can avoid a lot of anger, resentment, and misunderstandings with a regular dose of honesty.*

2. *Admit your mistakes.* If you make a mistake, admit it, do what you can to make amends, learn from it, and move on. You mustn't harbor guilt and destroy your confidence – that's going to get you nowhere, fast! *People trust and respect you more when you admit your mistakes and make things right.*

3. **Make others feel good about themselves.** Give sincere compliments and bring out their positive attributes. This, in turn, helps you feel good about yourself.

4. **Show your gratitude.** Everyone likes to be appreciated. Say *"thank you"* when someone has done something nice. They will reciprocate when you do something nice for them, thus boosting your own confidence.

5. **Follow the Golden Rule.** *Treat others the way you would like to be treated.* This builds your confidence because you're being true to yourself.

6. **Seek out others with these same qualities.** Your confidence will soar and your love will grow easily when you're dating someone on the same page as you.

7. **Focus on what you *do* have, not what you lack.** Oftentimes, people who've spend a long time searching for their soul-mate get discouraged because they *lack* that special partner. ***Instead of focusing on what you don't have, celebrate what you do have.***

   ❖ When you focus on your strengths, skills, and success, you're naturally gaining confidence. Why? Because your mind is centered on the positives in your life and positive attracts more positive!

Confidence is sexy, so if you have to fake confidence at first, so be it! At some point, that "fake" confidence will become a very real part of you!

Magnificent Confidence in Networking

Networking is the simple act of meeting other like-minded people.
The truth is, networking is critical to your success because you never know how valuable a new contact might be. Perhaps they'll become a business partner, a customer, or a wonderful new friend. But networking without self-confidence is tough!

When you *do* gain the confidence to network with others, you attract people to you like a magnet. This confidence allows you to focus more on the positive aspects of yourself and others. What happens is that people enjoy being around you because you make them feel as though they're valued and important.

A confident networker is able to build rock-solid foundations for both business and personal relationships, and it's easier than you think!

If you lack confidence in meeting others, try these tips:

4. **Prepare your elevator speech.** This is a concise, carefully planned 15-second description about what you do. The idea is to open up the conversation to more. It should be well-rehearsed, this way you're never caught off-guard when meeting new people.

    ❖ If you network for business purposes, your elevator speech should include something that makes them curious so they'll ask you for more if it piques their interest. For example, *"I show people how to pay off their mortgage in 15 years or less with no more money than they're spending now."*

    ❖ You should only continue talking about yourself if you're asked for more. The idea is to portray confidence, not arrogance, so be sure to ask others about what they do before rambling about your entire life story!

5. **Focus on others.** When you meet new people, focus on them and not yourself. People love talking about themselves. Allowing others to do so relieves you of any pressure to keep the conversation alive, instead, you can just listen and learn.

   ❖ The truth is, **people *love* people who *listen*.** Once you realize this and put it into action, networking will be a cinch and your confidence will skyrocket!

6. **Stay positive.** Bring up positive experiences and ideas. No one likes a *Debbie Downer.*

7. **Find common ground.** When you find similarities between you and the new person you just met, ***it brings you together.*** Your mutual fears are reduced because there's some common ground to explore.

8. **Look good.** When you know you look good, you feel confident about meeting others.

   ❖ *Be a sharp dresser.* Buy fewer clothes but spend more on each item. It will fit better, last longer, and look better than cheap clothing.

   ❖ *Stay in shape.* If you need to lose a few pounds, then design a nutrition and exercise plan that you know you can follow. Taking action will make you feel better about yourself when you meet new people. When you feel good about yourself, your confidence naturally improves.

9. **Don't worry what others think.** Worrying about what others think is *always* a losing battle. No human being is the judge of you. Do what you think is right and good and be proud of yourself!

Self-confidence plays a big part in networking, but first and foremost, you must ***know that you're unique and valuable.*** Treat yourself with love and respect, then others tend to follow suit. Soon you'll find that meeting new people becomes easier and easier and you'll *love* the new you!

Keep in mind, it is beauty INSIDE that counts more than anything. Confidence is a powerhouse of everything attractive and it comes from the INSIDE first.

Wellness Tips of the Week

Spontaneity creates excitement; excitement reminds us we're alive.

- ❖ Do something different, learn something new.
- ❖ Make use of all the wonderful tools out there to explore.
- ❖ Buy a book that teaches or informs about a topic you were always interested in.
- ❖ Join a new group you always wanted to join.

Go ahead step out of the box, do something different and joyful just for you.

This Week's Empowerment Tools

Inner Magnificence Diary

A great way to boost your confidence is to keep a magnificence diary.

It is a smart tool to just remind yourself just how good you really are and what you have to be thankful for and pleased about in your life right now.

Either get yourself a journal or notebook and once a week for the next month jot down your answers to the following confidence questions.

Don't make any excuses about why you haven't got the time to do it!

Take just 10 minutes per week, sit down and jot down your thoughts to:

1. **What have I got to be grateful for in my life right now?**

2. **What am I happy about in my life right now?**

3. **Why am I happy about these things?**

4. **What did I accomplish last week?**

5. **What am I excited about in my life right now?**

6. **Who do I love and appreciate in my life? Who do I like hanging around? Why?**

7. **Who loves and appreciates me for who I am?**

Answer these questions at the start of each week and it will set you up for success.

If you need a booster midweek, then by all means answer them again whenever you want to feel centered and remind yourself of what you have going for yourself in this moment in time.

Let's Keep in Touch...

My goal is to not have our connection broken at the end of this book, but rather to invite you to share your insight, thoughts and views on my "Goddess the Book" page, where you can download amazing empowering tools, which are hidden within the "Goddess Jewel Box" To join in, please go to www.facebook.com/goddessthebook or www.GoddessTheBook.com.

Sending out lots of Love, Joy and Happy energy to all,

Lori Snyder

About the Author

Lori Snyder is the outspoken creator of the recently launched "The Female Challenge" a core workout for mind, body and soul, focusing on the five cores of empowered success. She also wrote and facilitated the very powerful seminar/workshop "How to Stay Sane Before, During & After your Divorce" which helped many successfully move through this very transitional life change.

As a Speaker, Author, Occasional Cable TV Host/Anchor, former Dale Carnegie Consultant, and Certified Transition, Business and Lifestyle Coach, Lori is an expert in helping others discover their greatness. She is known for being on target in her coaching practice, and has a gift for being able to tap into her client's essence after knowing them for a short period of time.

Lori's focus is on integrating all core dimensions to help each person move into their most powerful, productive and successful state of well-being. She helps guide each person through the very things that are holding them back from achieving a life they love, and the happiness, success and joy they deserve.

Lori has been featured in More Magazine, where she was interviewed on her practices and thoughts toward achieving a healthy lifestyle, along with supreme balance to achieve optimal body, mind and soul.

She was also sought after by Wellness Magazine to act as their Life Coach for a six-month feature, where she was the exclusive Life-Stylist

Coach for six participants. Lori helped them create a life they loved through a six-month transitional journey, focusing on the individual needs of each person.

Lori has also written for many publications, both on and offline, including Generations Magazine, where she helped Senior's with transition. Lori enjoyed a seat on the board of the Long Island Professional Women's Association, and had an ongoing column in their monthly publication.

With a degree in Sociology and Anthropology, Lori has extensively studied psychology, sociology, philosophy and anthropology. She is also accredited and certified, both as a Certified Professional Coach (CPC) and an Energy Leadership Index™ Master Practitioner (ELI-MP).

Lori has a natural passion and love for her work. She enthusiastically helps her client's re-discover, re-define and re-create their life. she helps them to focus, establish and implement a plan of action, that will accept nothing less then their success.

Lori believes that the way one cultivates and cares for a relationship with themselves and with others is very important, along with how they nourish their body, mind and soul on a daily basis. She feels that each person holds within them powerful inner strength, that when tapped into can help them to create powerful, positive results towards making their lives an extraordinary one.

Lori is very active in various charities and is always open to learning more on how she can contribute and help others succeed in their life journey.